COOKING
a La
Nude

by
Bruce Carlson

Hearts & Tummies Cookbook Co.
a dinky division of Quixote Press

**3544 Blakslee St.
Wever, IA 52658
1-800-571-BOOK**

8th Printing

Hearts & Tummies Cookbook Co.
3544 Blakslee St.
Wever, IA 52658
1-800-571-BOOK

DEDICATION

This book is
fondly dedicated to Jane,
who taught me the
joys of cooking
in my birthday suit.

TABLE OF CONTENTS

FOREWORD

Bruce Carlson's light hearted approach to the subject of culinary pursuits a la nude will undoubtedly prove to be the definitive work in the subject for this, the latter years of the 20th century.

Prof. Damen Jewellston
Institute of Creative Cookery
Hanover University-SLR, Deu.

PREFACE

Cooking in the nude is not only iconoclastically meta-physical and presumptively irriguous of homogenous humanitarianism, but its a lot cooler on a hot day.

You heard it here first.

WHY?

o, what is it that would lead a person to do his or her cooking while nude? Why would he/she want to do that in the first place?

But, already in this very first sentence of this book, I have discovered a problem! And, that's the he/she problem. I'm gonna put that behind me right now. I'm not about to write a whole book with that he/she, him/her business. Not only is all that awfully awkward, but the / mark on my typewriter sticks a little bit. If I do a whole bunch of those he/shes and him/hers, my right hand pinkie is gonna give out.

So, what to do? I guess that no matter if I "he" my way through this book, or "she" my way through it, I'm gonna make a bunch of people mad at me.

Well, I guess the only answer is to use the female gender. For good or evil, the fact remains that most of the cooking done in America is done by females.

So, there!! It's she and her through and through ... like it or lump it!

But, back to the question at hand ... the question that is raised by the very title of this book. Why might a person be moved to do any cooking in the nude in the first place?

Well, there are reasons; in fact, quite a few of them.

One of them is forgetfulness. Let's fact it, we women are burdened with a just plain awful number of responsibilities these days. All those gotta-do's can get to weighing

heavily on our minds, even as early as when we first get up in the morning. So, it's easy to get up, thinking about all that, and just plain forget to get dressed before tackling the affairs of the day.

I'm not saying that a woman's going to forget to get herself dressed just every day that comes along, but she will do so on occasions. Sometimes you've gotten through breakfast, gotten the kids delivered to school or day care or wherever they have to go, and had a good start on that get-the-day-going cup of coffee ... before you've suddenly realize you are still as naked as a jay bird.

That's just the way some days go, you know.

Then, there are things like discovering, in the morning that you just "don't have a thing to wear."

And, how about air conditioners? Everybody knows that an air conditioner won't break down on those sort of in-between days. They always pick the hottest day of the year to blow a motor or lose a belt. Some folks have allergies to fabrics. Sometimes these can be so bad that it's easier to go without clothes than to fight the allergy.

And, how about political statements? It's the fashion to make political statements by takin' all your clothes off, you know. Folks aren't gonna give up thinkin' politics jus' cause other folks expect 'em to wear clothes all the time.

Then, lastly, how about nudists? They don't spend all their time doin' exercises and soakin' up sunshine you know. They have chores to do, includin' cookin'.

Come to think of it, there're probably more reasons to do your cookin' a la nude than there are to do it with clothes on.

So, that's the "why" of it. The rest of this book will be devoted to some so-good-they'll-knock-your-socks-off recipes and some practical guidance on cooking in the nude. Between these pages you'll find some awfully useful information and helpful hints about the art of cooking in your birthday suit.

... come to think of it, let's go back a paragraph or two so's we can change that ... "it'll knock your socks off" ... to ... "they're just really fine" ... I mean ... that is to say, if you're nude there's nothing that's gonna knock your

socks ... I mean, you already don't have any socks ... really, don't have anything at all ... well, anyway, it's not all that important.

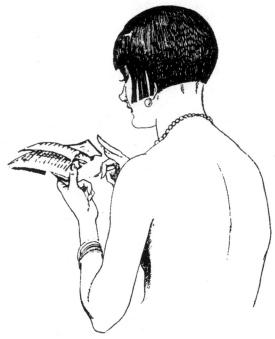

APPETIZERS

&

BEVERAGES

CHEESE SPREAD

¼ lb. butter or oleo   1 lb. Velveeta cheese
3 oz. pkg. cream cheese   1 C. ground pecans
2 T. dry garlic
    Blend and roll into shapes you desire in chili powder. This freezes nicely.

PIMENTO CHEESE FOR SANDWICH FILLING

2 eggs, beaten   ⅔ C. vinegar
¾ C. sugar   1 lb. Longhorn cheese, ground
2 T. flour   1 can pimento peppers
2 T. margarine
    Cook eggs, sugar, flour and vinegar until thick in heavy saucepan. When thick add 2 T. margarine. Mix dressing with ground cheese and pimentos. Add a little cream or milk.

PUNCH (Serves 35)

4 pkg. Kool-Aid
2 C. sugar
3½ qt. water
1 can frozen lemonade

1 can frozen orange juice
1 large can pineapple juice
1 large bottle gingerale or 7-Up

Use kind of Kool-Aid according to the color of punch desired. It is best to dissolve sugar and water over low heat, then cool. Add gingerale or 7-Up just before serving.

BANANA SLUSH

1 large can pineapple juice
1 large can orange juice
5 bananas

6 C. water
1 C. sugar
Juice of 2 lemons

Heat water and sugar until dissolved. Put lemon juice in blender then bananas to liquify. Mix all juices and bananas mixture together and freeze. Thaw 3-4 hours before serving and add gingerale or 7-Up. Put in blender to mix.

FRUIT SLUSH

1 6-oz. can frozen lemonade
1 6-oz. can frozen orange juice
1 8-oz. pkg. frozen strawberries
  (slightly thawed & cut in ¼ths)
2 #2 cans crushed pineapple (undrained)

1 4-oz. can maraschino cherries
  (drained, blotted & cut in ½)
4 or 5 sliced bananas
4 C. water
2 C. sugar

Stir all together and put in individual cups and freeze. Fills about 14 to 16 9-oz. cups. Let thaw about 45 minutes at room temperature, or defrost in microwave 30-45 seconds before serving.

WHITE PUNCH (Serves 75)

1 gallon pkg. Wylers lemonade mix
1 gallon water
4 C. sugar
1 46-oz. can pineapple juice

1 46-oz. pineapple-grapefruit juice
3 T. pineapple sherbet
1 C. 7-Up
1 C. gingerale

Use the first ingredients for the ice ring. Put the 3 T. sherbet in the bottom of the punch bowl.

CRAB ROLL-UP

½ lb. Velveeta cheese
½ lb. butter (2 sticks)
20 slices white bread

1 C. sesame seed
1 can (7 oz.) crab meat

Melt 1 stick oleo in cheese. Cool and add meat. Cut crusts off bread and roll flat. Spread with mixture and roll; freeze. Thaw slightly and cut into 3rds. Melt 1 stick oleo and dunk in. Roll in seeds and broil until brown. Turn once.

FRENCH BREAD SPREAD

1 C. Hellman's mayonnaise
½ C. Parmesan cheese

½ med. sized onion, chopped fine
½ tsp. Worcestershire sauce

Cut bread lengthwise. Spread with 1 C. soft butter. Wrap in foil and heat thoroughly. Remove from oven. Spread mixture over it. Put under broiler until bubbly and brown. Slice into serving pieces.

VEGETABLE DIP

1 C. mayonnaise　　　　　　　　　1 tsp. curry powder
1 tsp. instant onion salt　　　　　　1 tsp. tarragon vinegar
1 tsp. garlic salt　　　　　　　　　1 tsp. horseradish
　　Mix all together and serve with raw vegetables.

HOT HAMBURGER DIP

1½ lb. hamburger　　　　　　　　1 can Cheddar cheese soup
½ lb. Velveeta cheese　　　　　　　1 small can green chilies
1 onion　　　　　　　　　　　　　1 jar taco sauce
1 can refried beans
　　Brown hamburger and onion together. Add rest in crock pot on low heat. Heat until cheese is melted. Serve with Nacho cheese chips.

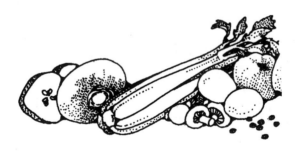

VEGETABLE DIP

1 C. mayonnaise　　　　　　　　　2 T. milk
½-1 tsp. ginger　　　　　　　　　2 T. minced onion (dry flake)
4 tsp. soy sauce　　　　　　　　　1 tsp. vinegar
　　Mix all together and refrigerate. Good with raw vegetables or potato chips. Makes approximately 1 cup. Keeps three weeks.

EARL THARP'S MARGARITAS

TO MAKE 1 GALLON:
16 oz. triple sec   24 oz. tequila
22 oz. port-a-call*   66 oz. water

TO MAKE 2 QUARTS:
8 oz. triple sec   12 oz. tequila
11 oz. port-a-call*   33 oz. water

TO MAKE 1 QUART:
4 oz. triple sec   6 oz. tequila
5½ oz. port-a-call*   16½ oz. water

TO MAKE 1 PINT:
2 oz. triple sec   3 oz. tequila
2¾ oz. port-a-call*   8¼ oz. water

*SWEET AND SOUR MIX:
¼ C. = 2 oz.   ⅔ C. = 5½ oz.
⅓ C. = 2¾ oz.   ¾ C. = 6 oz.
½ C. = 4 oz.   1 C. = 8 oz.

BEER BATTER FOR FISH

1 C. flour   1 egg
1 can beer   1 tsp. baking powder
1 tsp. salt

Mix together and dip fish.

PICKLED NORTHERN (Fish)

1 qt. white vinegar
2 large onions (cut up)
1½ oz. pickling spice
Raw fish (cut up)

1 qt. cold water
1½ oz. pickling salt
1½ C. sugar

Mix in gallon jar. Add enough pieces of fish to fill jar. Stand at room temperature for 48 hours, then refrigerate. Turn jar a couple times to stir contents during the 48 hours. This keeps several months. Bones will soften and not be a problem.

CRACKIDILLY MIX

2 pkgs. small oyster crackers
1 pkg. Hidden Valley Ranch (dry)
harvest onion home style mix

1 C. Wesson Oil
1 T. (scant) dill weed

Mix together and spread on cookie sheets and place in oven (250°) for 3-5 minutes. Cool and store in tight containers.

BRANDY SLUSH

9 C. water
2 C. sugar
1 (12 oz.) can frozen lemonade

1 (12 oz.) can frozen orange juice
1 pint brandy

Boil water and sugar until sugar dissolves. Let cool ½ hour. Add lemonade, orange juice, and brandy. Put in ice cream pail or large container. Freeze. Put 2 scoops in glass and fill with 7-Up.

CITRUS PUNCH

3 (6 oz. ea.) cans frozen orange juice
3 (6 oz. ea.) cans frozen lemonade
2 C. sugar

2 qts. water
1 (46 oz.) can pineapple juice
2 (2-liter ea.) bottles ginger ale

NOTE: Makes better punch when the water, pineapple juice, and the ginger ale are chilled.

FROZEN DAIQUIRI

1/5th white rum	1 (12 oz.) can lemonade
1 (6 oz.) can frozen lemonade	5 C. water (not lemon juice)
(not lime juice)	

Stir altogether in a large mixing bowl or container. Freeze for 10 hours, then stir until slushy. Return to freezer until ready to serve, then stir before serving. (I put a couple drops of green food coloring in mine to make it look more festive, optional.) Garnish with maraschino cherry.

HAM SALAD

½-¾ lb. bologna	8 oz. spiced ham
8 oz. family loaf	2-3 hard boiled eggs
Sweet pickle relish and juice	Mustard
Miracle Whip	

Grind and mix meat. Mix pickle juice, sugar, mustard, and Miracle Whip Add all ingredients together. Chop eggs and add. Mix well.

SNAX

1-2 pkgs. pretzels	2 lbs. salted mixed nuts
1 pkg. Cheerios	2 T. Worcestershire sauce
1 pkg. Wheat Chex	½ T. garlic salt
1 pkg. Rice Chex	1 T. seasoned salt
1 pkg. Corn Chex	2 C. salad oil

Mix all seasonings with oil. Then mix in other ingredients, putting Rice Chex in last. Bake at 200° for 2 hours, tossing every 15 minutes. Enough for 8 or 9 one-lb. coffee cans. Best in the land!

Not Bringin' Home the Bacon

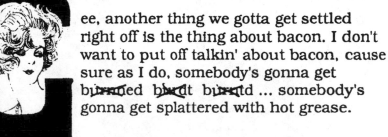

ee, another thing we gotta get settled right off is the thing about bacon. I don't want to put off talkin' about bacon, cause sure as I do, somebody's gonna get b~~urned~~ b~~urt~~ b~~urntd~~ ... somebody's gonna get splattered with hot grease.

I know this doesn't look like most pigs you might be used to, but this is how the porkers in our neighborhood look ever since they built that nuclear power plant just upriver a few miles.*

It isn't the bacon itself so much as it's the fryin' of the bacon. The bacon itself is as harmless as an old shoe. It's when you get to fryin' it that you can really get into trouble.

*If you kind of squint your eyes a little, it'll look more piglike

You might not know about all this, but the whole mess goes back many many centuries, back when someone foolishly did something to tick off some ancient Grecian or Roman Goddess.

This particular goddess is The Goddess of Itty Bitty Flyin' Things.

The GOIBFT has still got a thing in her craw about that thing, whatever it was, that somebody did back then.

Not only is she still mad about that, but she's still takin' it out on folks. Mainly she does that with fryin' bacon and grapefruit halves.

You already know about the grapefruit halves, of course. You can get all primed up to poke a spoon into half a

grapefruit, and fool yourself into thinking you're gonna outwit it this time. You can squint your eyes so's they's just teeny tiny little slits to see out of. You can go ahead

and do that, but, down deep, you still know exactly
what's gonna happen. That little squirt of juice could
head on out toward the window, aim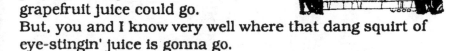
for the refrigerator, or
for that whole row of
cabinets. Or, for that
matter, it could just plain
light anywhere it wanted
to out on the floor. There
are literally thousands ...
tens of thousands of
places that squirt of
grapefruit juice could go.
But, you and I know very well where that dang squirt of
eye-stingin' juice is gonna go.

Your doin' all that eye squirtin' is gonna getcha nowhere. All that does is to make that stream of juice
focus its aim a little more carefully ... and you're gonna
get it IN THE EYE.

It's that dang Goddess of Itty Bitty Flyin' Things doin'
her dirty work again!

But, let's back up a little bit here! We were talkin' fryin'
bacon. That's the stuff I wanted to warn you about in
this chapter.

The GOIBFT, no doubt, enjoys splattering all over the
just-cleaned kitchen curtains, and making a mess

out of the counters and cabinets with that dang bacon grease, but she gets her biggest jollies from doing the really nasty stuff.

The GOIBFT gets a special kick out of splattering out as fast as its little legs 'll carry it.

That's just the kind of Goddess she is.

But curtains and cats aside, the GOIBFT enjoys mostly splattering that hot grease onto humans.

And, of course, the hotter the grease is, the better, according to that dang goddess. But, the ideal situation is when the grease is hotter'n all get out, and the human is in her birthday suit.

'Cause, it's when the fry cook's got her birthday suit on that makes it perfect. You see, runnin' around in the nude sort of does an industrial strength job of exposing tender parts to the elements.

Now, we're all grown-up folks here, so I'm not gonna go into all kinds of details about how bein' in the nude goes about exposing particularly tender spots an' all, but it does.

And the GOIBFT will see to it that those tender spots will get the full attention of those hot little splatters of grease from fryin' bacon.

CANDY

&

COOKIES

CHIP COOKIES

1 C. brown sugar
1 C. white sugar
1 C. margarine
1 C. salad oil
1 egg
2 tsp. vanilla
3½ C. flour
1 tsp. salt

1 tsp. soda
1 tsp. cream of tartar
1 C. coconut
1 C. oats
1 C. Rice Krispies
1 C. nuts
1 C. chocolate or butterscotch chips

Cream sugars and margarine. Add remaining ingredients. Drop by teaspoon. Bake at 350° for 12 to 15 minutes.

APPLESAUCE OATMEAL COOKIES

½ C. margarine
½ C. Crisco
½ C. brown sugar
½ C. white sugar
1 C. unsweetened applesauce
2 eggs
2 tsp. vanilla

1 tsp. salt
1 tsp. soda
¼ tsp. cinnamon
¼ tsp. nutmeg
2¼ C. flour
2 C. oatmeal
Raisins & nuts totaling 1 C.

Cream margarine and Crisco. Add sugars, applesauce, eggs and vanilla. Beat with mixer for 2 minutes. Gradually add salt, soda, spices and flour that has been sifted together. Stir in oatmeal, raisins and nuts, (I use half black walnuts and half raisins). Bake at 350°. Drop from spoon on cookie sheet. Yields 4 dozen cookies.

COCOA DROPS

½ C. shortening (soft) part butter
1 C. sugar
1 egg
¾ C. buttermilk or sour milk
1 tsp. vanilla

1¾ C. sifted flour
½ tsp. soda
½ C. cocoa
½ tsp. salt
1 C. chopped nuts (optional)

Mix shortening, sugar and egg thoroughly. Stir in buttermilk or sour milk and vanilla. Mix dry ingredients together and stir in. Add nuts, if desired. Chill 1 hour. Heat oven to 375°. Drop dough by teaspoon 2 inches apart onto lightly greased cookie sheet. Bake about 8 minutes. Don't overbake. Cool and frost.

CHRISTMAS ROCKS

1 C. butter
¾ C. brown sugar
¾ C. white sugar
3 eggs
2½ C. flour
1 tsp. cinnamon
1 tsp. salt
1 tsp. soda

1 lb. dates
12 oz. white raisins
8 oz. red candied cherries
1½ C. candied pineapple
8 oz. English walnuts, halved
4 oz. blanched split almonds
8 oz. Brazil nuts (large)
8 oz. halved pecans

Add eggs, 1 at a time to the butter and sugars. Combine flour, cinnamon, salt and soda. Save 1 cup of the flour mixture before combing to butter mix. Cut up fine the fruits and nuts in a pan. Sift the 1 cup flour mixture over fruit and nut mixture. Mix well. Pour batter over fruit and nut mix. Whip ¼ C. cream and add 1 tsp. vanilla. Fold whipped cream into mixture. Drop by teaspoon on oiled cookie sheet. Bake at 350° for 10 minutes. Makes 150 cookies.

CARAMELS

1 C. sugar	1 C. light cream
¾ C. dark corn syrup	½ C. chopped nuts
½ C. butter or margarine	

Butter sides of heavy 2 quart saucepan. In it combine sugar, corn syrup, butter and ½ C. cream. Bring to boiling over low heat, stirring constantly. Slowly stir in remaining ½ cup of cream. Cook over low heat to medium ball stage (242°), stirring almost constantly toward the end. Remove from heat and add nuts (I prefer black walnuts) and vanilla. Pour into buttered 9 x 5 x 3-inch pan. Mark in 32 squares, when partially cool. Cut when cold and wrap, store in airtight container.

PEANUT BUTTER CUPS CANDY

⅓ lb. graham cracker crumbs	1 lb. powdered sugar
½ lb. oleo	2 C. chocolate chips
1 C. peanut butter	

Combine crumbs, oleo, peanut butter and sugar. Work until smooth. Press mixture into buttered 9 x 9-inch (or a little larger) pan. Melt chips over hot water and spread over cracker mixture. Refrigerate until firm, cut in squares. (This candy tastes like peanut butter cups sold under the brand name.)

DIVINITY

2½ C. granulated sugar	2 egg whites
½ C. corn syrup	1 C. nutmeats
½ C. water	1 tsp. vanilla

Combine the sugar, corn syrup and water. Cook until it spins a thread (238°). Pour half the syrup over the two stiffly-beaten egg whites. Return the remaining syrup to range and cook to the hardball stage. When tested in water, should sort of crack against side of cup. Pour slowly over egg whites and beat until it stands in peaks. Add the vanilla and nutmeats. Drop by teaspoonfuls on waxed paper. Place bowl in hot water while dropping the candy or if it becomes too firm to drop add a little hot water to it. May add a little food coloring if desired. Makes 60 pieces.

MORE PRECAUTIONS

ee here now, I'd be the last person in the world to discourage folks from cooking in the nude, but I would ask you to be aware of some little things that are relatively harmless when you are wearing clothes, but become downright serious when you're cooking in your birthday suit.

Consider, for example, those little globs of hot gravy that land on a blouse or on a sleeve when you are pouring it

from the pan into the bowl. Your sleeve won't blister, and your blouse won't turn red, ... but you do.

And those half dozen remaining chocolate chips that are too many to throw away, and too few to save. You know very well what happens to them. You pop 'em in your mouth and eat 'em.

Then, along about two or three minutes later, they end up there on your hips, even magnified in weight, so proud they are of finding your hips so quickly, seein' as how it's so dark inside, and everything takin' all those twists and turns ... Fact is, scientific analysis reinforced with mononuclear spectrographic chromatography has shown that one ounce of chocolate chips will yield one and a half ounces of flab ... on each hip!

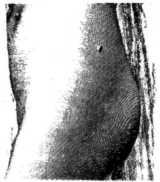

Well, of course, cooking without any clothes on won't make the whole chocolate chip situation any worse than if you were cooking fully dressed, it just makes it more visible right away.

There is hope, however. There is an answer to the problem of the effects of gobblin' down those end-of-the-package chocolate chips. The answer is fiendishly clever if you think about it. All you have to do is to reduce the number of packages that come to the end of. If you have only one package in a year's time to ponder over what to do with those last half dozen chips, instead of a number of times, you are gonna gobble 'em down a lot fewer times.

If everything worked out according to theory, you should end up bein' a pretty skinny individual after a while of employing that little scheme.

I have a cousin who put that plan into action. Instead of facing the issue of how to handle those last few chips every couple of weeks or every month or so, she bought her chocolate chips by the trunkful.

That way, the only times she was faced with that small handful of left over chips was after she had used a whole trunkful of 'em.

That cousin of mine is just real proud of her cleverness in handling that situation. And, hardly anybody notices the three pieces of four-in I-beams they built into the frame of her bed to hold her up.

BREADS

CAKE ROLLS

2½ C. warm water   2 pkg. yeast
1 reg. yellow cake mix   4½ C. flour
   Mix and knead. Let rise to double. Roll into rectangle (a third or half at a time).
Spread as for cinnamon rolls, using butter, white or brown sugar and cinnamon.
Let rise to double. Bake at 350° for 15-20 minutes.

KOLACHES

2 pkg. dry yeast   ½ C. warm water
1 tsp. sugar   1 C. milk
½ C. water   ½ C. sugar
½ C. soft shortening   1 T. salt
6-7 C. flour   2 eggs
   Mix yeast, warm water and 1 tsp. sugar and let set until it bubbles; scald milk.
When cooled, stir in yeast mixture. Then add 2 beaten eggs and mix well. Add
2 cups of flour and beat until smooth. Keep adding flour and mix until stiff enough
to knead. Knead until smooth and put in greased bowl. Cover and put in warm
place until double in volume. Roll out ½-inch and cut in any size. Brush with butter
and let rise until double. Make an impression in center of dough the size you want
and add fruit mixture. Bake in 375° oven for 15-20 minutes. Fruit mixture: Cook
apricots, prunes, dates, etc. with water until done. Pour off water and sweeten
fruit to taste. Makes a thick paste.

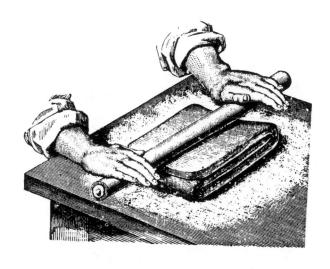

DATE BREAD

1 C. dates	1 tsp. soda
1 C. sugar	1 T. fat, lard or Crisco
½ tsp. salt	1 C. boiling water
2 C. flour	½ C. walnuts
1 egg	½ tsp. vanilla

Pour water over dates (cut in small pieces). Add sugar, shortening and salt. Let cool. Stirring occasionally, add remaining ingredients. Add well beaten egg. Mix thoroughly and bake in a greased bread pan at 350° for 45 minutes to 1 hour. Sides should shrink from sides and is browned.

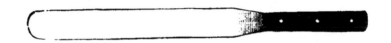

CRANBERRY BREAD

2 C. chopped cranberries	¾ C. walnuts
2 T. melted butter	2 C. flour
1 C. & 2 T. sugar	1¾ tsp. baking powder
1 tsp. salt	1 egg
¼ C. water	½ C. orange juice
1 tsp. orange rind	

Combine egg, water and orange juice in small bowl. Add melted butter to liquid ingredients. Add liquid to combined dry ingredients. Stir only until moistened. Add nuts, orange rind and cranberries. Bake at 350° for 70 minutes. Makes 2 loaves.

LEMON BREAD

1 pkg. lemon cake mix	½ C. cooking oil
1 pkg. instant lemon pudding	1 C. water
4 eggs	1/8 C. poppy seed

Mix with electric beater until blended. Bake 40 minutes at 350° in two 8 x 3-inch loaf pans, greased and floured.

SQUASH BREAD

1½ C. flour	2 tsp. cinnamon
1 tsp. baking powder	½ tsp. baking soda
¼ tsp. salt	2 eggs
¾ C. sugar	½ C. oil
2 tsp. vanilla	1⅓ C. summer squash, shredded

Preheat oven to 350°. Grease a 9 x 5 x 3-inch loaf pan. Mix dry ingredients, except sugar thoroughly. Beat eggs until frothy. Add sugar, oil and vanilla. Beat until lemon colored, about 3 minutes. Stir in squash. Add dry ingredients. Mix just until dry ingredients are moistened. Pour into loaf pan. Bake 40 minutes or until toothpick inserted in center of loaf comes out clean. Cool on rack. Remove from pan after 10 minutes. Note: Zucchini or yellow summer squash may be used.

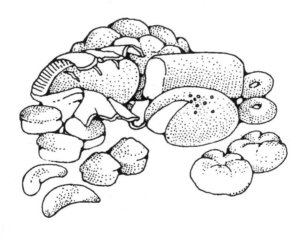

REFRIGERATOR ROLLS

2 pkg. dry yeast	1 tsp. sugar
½ C. warm water	Dash ginger
1 C. warm water ·	½ C. melted shortening
½ C. sugar	1 tsp. salt
3 beaten eggs	5 C. flour

Dissolve yeast in ½ C. warm water. Add sugar and ginger. Combine 1 cup water, shortening, sugar, salt and eggs. Add yeast mixture. Stir in 3 cups flour and beat with mixer until smooth. Gradually add rest of flour to make stiff dough (by hand). Turn onto floured board. Knead until smooth & satiny. Store covered in refrigerator at least 2½ hours. Overnight is best. Punch down at least once during this time. Shape into rolls and let rise in warm place 2½ hours or until double. Bake at 375°. Good for dinner rolls, braided or bread doughnuts. 4 dozen rolls.

OLA'S HOT ROLL SPECIAL

1 C. hot water	1 rounded T. shortening
½ C. sugar	1 large egg
1 tsp. salt	4 C. flour
1 pkg. yeast	¼ C. warm water

Dissolve yeast in warm water. Pour hot water in bowl. Add shortening and sugar. Stir until lukewarm, then add eggs, salt and 3 cups flour. Then beat, beat, beat - the more the better. Add yeast and remaining flour and beat some more. Let rise until double. Punch down and divide in 3 parts. Roll in circle, cover with melted butter and cut into 8 pieces. Roll toward the point. Let rise and bake at 375°.

ORANGE STICKY BUNS

⅓ C. honey   1 T. honey
¼ C. orange juice concentrate   ½ tsp. cinnamon
¾ C. brown sugar   ½ C. nuts
2 tubes biscuits

Place honey in round pan. Melt butter and add orange juice. In another bowl combine the brown sugar and cinnamon. Dip first in butter and juice, then in the sugar mixture. Stand biscuits on edge in the pan. Bake at 375° for 30 minutes. Cool 15 minutes and serve warm.

ANGEL BISCUIT

1 pkg. dry yeast   1/8 C. sugar
¼ C. warm water   ½ C. shortening
2½ C. flour   1 C. buttermilk
½ tsp. baking powder   1 tsp. salt

Dissolve yeast in warm water; set aside. Mix dry ingredients in order given, cutting in the shortening as you normally do for biscuits. Stir in buttermilk and yeast mixture. Blend thoroughly. Dough is now ready to refrigerate or roll out as biscuits. When you are ready to make these delicious biscuits, turn the dough out onto a floured board and knead lightly. Roll out and cut with a biscuit cutter, placing them on a greased pan. Let dough rise slightly before baking in a 400° oven for 12 to 15 minutes, until browned. If dough is cold you will need to let it rise longer.

BRAN MUFFINS

15 oz. box Raisin Bran   1 C. oil
3 C. sugar   4 eggs
1 qt. buttermilk   5 C. flour
5 tsp. baking soda   2 tsp. salt

Put all ingredients into ice cream bucket and store in refrigerator until ready to bake. Makes a lot. Bake at 400° for 20-30 minutes. Can add dates if desired. Keeps several weeks.

EASY ROLLS OR BUNS

2 pkg. dry yeast	½ C. warm water
2 C. hot water	2 tsp. salt
½ C. sugar	3 T. butter (don't substitute)
6-6½ C. flour	

Dissolve yeast in warm water. Pour hot water over sugar and butter. Add 2 C. flour, beating hard after each addition and when mixture is warm, not hot; add dissolved yeast. Then add balance of flour to which salt has been added. Knead well and place in greased bowl; let rise until double in bowl. Shape into rolls or buns. Let rise until double. Bake at 375° for about 20 minutes. Grease tops with butter.

CHEESE FRENCH BREAD

1 loaf French bread	½ C. soft butter
1 C. Hellman's mayonnaise	½ C. Parmesan cheese
½ of med. onion, chopped fine	½ T. Worcestershire sauce

Cut bread lengthwise and spread with butter. Wrap in foil and heat about 10 minutes. Open flat and spread on top mixture of mayonnaise Parmesan cheese, onion and Worcestershire sauce. Put on cookie sheet leaving open and broil until bubbly.

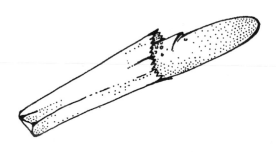

CINNAMON ROLLS

2 C. warm water
⅔ C. shortening
2 tsp. salt
¾ C. sugar

⅓ C. dry milk
2 beaten eggs
5½-6 C. flour

    Beat together and let rise 1 hour. Pat down and roll out and spread with butter. Sprinkle brown sugar, zig-zag dark Karo syrup and half and half and sprinke pecans on bottom of pan before putting rolls in. Let rise. Bake at 350° for 20-25 minutes.

BAKING POWDER BISCUITS

2 C. flour
1 tsp. salt
¾ C. milk (about)

4 tsp. baking powder
4 T. shortening

    Sift flour with baking powder and salt. Cut in shortening until mixture is the consistency of cornmeal; add milk and mix quickly to soft dough. Knead until smooth; pat or roll to ½-inch thick. Cut with biscuit cutter, place on greased baking pan. Bake preheated oven of 450°-475° for 12-15 minutes or until light brown. Yield 12-18 biscuits.

BROWN 'N SERVE PIZZA

1 C. warm water	1 pkg. dry yeast
1 T. sugar	1½ tsp. salt
2 T. oil	2¾-3¼ C. flour

Measure water into large bowl and sprinkle in yeast. Stir until dissolved. Stir in sugar, salt, oil and 1½ C. of flour. Beat until smooth. Add remaining flour to make a stiff dough. Turn onto lightly floured board and knead about five minutes. Place in greased bowl, cover and let rise in a warm place until doubled about 45 minutes. Punch down, divide in half. Roll and stretch each into 13'' round or oblong to fit cookie sheet (ungreased). Bake at 350° for 10 minutes. When cool wrap tightly and store in refrigerator up to 6 days. Keeps indefinitely in freezer. To serve, place on ungreased pan, top any way desired. Bake at 425° for 20 minutes.

NO DRY NOODLES

4 eggs	4 T. cooking oil
1 tsp. salt	¼ tsp. baking powder
Flour	

Combine ingredients using enough flour to make a stiff dough. Roll out, cut and add to broth.

BUTTERMILK PANCAKES

1 C. flour	1 tsp. baking powder
½ tsp. baking soda	½ tsp. salt
1 T. sugar	1 egg
3 T. oil	1 C. buttermilk

Mix dry ingredients. Add egg, buttermilk and oil; mix quickly.

POTATO DOUGHNUTS

2 T. butter	1⅓ C. sugar
½ tsp. salt	1 C. milk
½ tsp. vanilla	3 eggs
1 C. hot mashed potatoes	4 C. sifted flour
2 T. baking powder	2 tsp. nutmeg

Add butter, sugar, milk and beaten eggs to mashed potatoes. Mix well and gradually add the sifted dry ingredients. Add vanilla; chill dough for 2 hours. Then roll about ⅓-inch thick. Cut and fry in deep fat heated, to 375° until puffed and golden brown. Turn just once. Roll in granulated sugar.

STICKIE QUICKIE BUNS

1½ C. flour
¾ C. milk
¼ C. butter
1 tsp. salt
1¾ C. flour

2 pkg. yeast
½ C. water
¼ C. sugar
1 egg

TOPPING:
¾ C. butter
1 tsp. cinnamon
1 T. corn syrup

1 C. brown sugar
¾ C. nuts
1 T. water

Combine the 1½ cups of flour and yeast. Heat the milk, water, butter, sugar and salt until warm (120°). Pour into yeast mixture; add egg, beat on high speed of mixer for 3 minutes. By hand stir in 1¾ cups flour. Cover and let rise for 30 minutes. While dough is rising combine the topping ingredients in a saucepan and heat until melted. Pour in a 9 x 13-inch pan. Stir down batter and drop by tablespoons on topping. Bake at 375° for 20 minutes. Cool 1 minute and invert on cookie sheet.

CINNAMON MUFFINS

¼ C. butter
½ C. sugar
1 egg
1½ C. flour
2 tsp. baking powder

¼ tsp. salt
½ C. milk
⅓ C. melted butter
Cinnamon & sugar
½ tsp. nutmeg

Cream shortening and sugar. Add egg yolk and beat well. Add the sifted dry ingredients, alternating with milk. Fold in stiffly beaten egg white. Fill well-greased muffin tins ⅔ full. Bake at 350° for 20-25 minutes. When baked, quickly roll muffins in melted butter and cinnamon-sugar mixture.

Stung in a Sting

H ow about Mrs. George McPhillips, wife of State's Attorney McPhillips, who learned a lesson the hard way one day?

What the whole thing boiled down to was that she learned that what seemed to be harmless little circumstances can conspire to end up with far reaching, and unfortunate effects.

Mrs. McPhillips was of a mind, now and then, to do her cooking in the nude. It wasn't any big deal with Evelyn, just a harmless little indulgence she allowed herself on occasion.

It was in February, not too long before Valentine's Day when the thought occurred to her that she might make her young granddaughters some valentine cookies ... you know, the tasteless little kind with gritty stuff on 'em ... the cookies, not the granddaughters.

So, that's what she did. Her husband was gone for the day, the nosey neighbor next door who had the habit of sticking her head in the back door with a neighborly YOO-HOO was safely in the hospital having a gall bladder operation. The girls were in school and her

husband's friend, who often came to the house was busy working on some sort of secret police operation. He was a good hundred miles away coordinating some doings with a regional law enforcement committee.

All in all, it was a sort of ideal day for some baking sans clothes.

So, off went the clothes, and out came the makings of some valentine cookies. In addition to all the ingredients, there were bowls, the mixer, and the cookie cutters. Oh, such an array of cookie cutters. There were

cupids and hearts. There were bunnies and snowmen. There were all kinds of fun cookie cutters, suitable for all kinds of holidays. And the holiday coming up real soon was a really great one with the children ... it was going to be Valentine's Day!

The thought of those shiny little faces, and fat little hands made Evelyn smile as she flitted around in the kitchen ... flitting around, incidentally, in her all together.

The more Evelyn thought about the situation, the more she realized she wasn't going to get by with making just a couple dozen cookies. Not only were there the three granddaughters, but one of them was fixing to have a party, and could well use some extra cookies for that.

Then, there would be the cookies swiped by some hungry Daddies, and the neighbor boy who would want some. He was a rowdy kid, but likeable. Not only all that, but those girls would be wanting to take some with them in their lunches to school.

Evelyn got to addin' up all those people, and realized she would have to make at least twelve dozen of those cookies to make everybody happy.

By the time Evelyn got all that mixing and cutting out done, and the baking and lettin' 'em cool, she was one tired-out lady.

Evelyn knew that when she once got to sit down, she wouldn't be in the mood to get up and finish the job, so she drove herself to complete that very last cookie and to clean up the kitchen well before she allowed herself the luxury of a rest.

Finally, after the last bowl was cleaned and the last cookie set out to cool, she pulled out a kitchen chair and plopped down like she was never going to get up again until at least the middle of December when it would be time to start the Christmas cookies.

But, she got up again in about a thousandths of a second. She suddenly regained enough strength to come roarin' up outta that chair like she'd been stabbed.

And, that, in fact ...is exactly what she had been. There, embedded in Evelyn's left cheek, was a heart shaped cookie cutter. Of course, that dang thing had to land sharp side up when it slipped off the table and had landed on that chair! She really got it good!

Talk about hurt!! It was a good old-fashioned bringin'-tears-to-the-eyes kind of hurt. The hurt outlasted the time it took to extract the offending cookie cutter. It outlasted the puttin'-stuff-on-it-in-the-mirror-backwards as she tried to get the wound coated with iodine. It outlasted the additional hurt from the iodine that tastefully outlined the heart. It outlasted the little lecture the attorney general delivered, upon his return, on the folly of cooking in the nude.

After the hurt was finally gone, there was still a heart-shaped wound on Evelyn's south end, well, and permanently outlined by the iodine. After about two weeks the wound was gone, but the darkened scar remained.

Evelyn found that the scar was low enough on her south end that her clothes did a pretty good job of hiding it. That is, they did except when her sweater would sort of work up, and her skirt sort of scootched down.

And, that's exactly what happened on the McPhillips' thirty-fifth wedding anniversary when they were eating out in a restaurant in the neighboring town.

Neither Evelyn nor her husband realized that that particular restaurant had fallen onto disreputable times. They didn't know about the various projects a local vice operator had going there in what had been a nice respectable restaurant in a nice respectable neighborhood.

Nor did they know about the sting operation that was planned for that very nightspot that evening. It all came as a real surprise to both of them.

 Evelyn did mention later, that she had begun to notice that several of the younger ladies seemed to be dressed rather suggestively. In fact, she said, she was just leaning over to make mention of one girl in particular, to her husband. She was going to point out that this one girl seemed to have little on other than a short leather thing and some fishnet hose.

It was, just as she was leaning over to tell him about all that, when pandomonium broke loose.

Before anyone could say, "Check, please," there were wall-to-wall cops guarding all the exits and shaking folks down. Suddenly, out of nowhere, there were half a dozen lady cops, questioning the women. They seemed to be sorting out those with provocative clothes, sporting tattoos, or otherwise suggesting that things were not totally on the up and up.

It was probably all this excitement and the twisting around to see what was going on that caused Evelyn's sweater to work up a little bit and for her skirt to slip down just a smidgeon there in the back.

But, that smidgeon was enough to expose just a little bit

of that fetching little heart-shaped image on her left cheek.

Well, now, those lady cops knew all about fishnet hose, leather skirts, and tattoos ... even if this particular sexy little number was almost invisible, down below that skirt ... just a cute little bit of it playfully peeking out from under that skirt.

Before you could say, "But...," Evelyn found herself lined up at the bar right between a gal wearing only a boa wrap and a smile and another gal with a Harley Davidson tattoo on her right shoulder.

This account of the trials of Mrs. McPhillips is getting too long now, so I won't go into all the sordid details about what happened. But, I can tell you that the news of the incident swept through the Republican Party headquarters down on Third Avenue like wildfire.

While the whole ugly incident was eventually put behind the McPhillips, Mrs. McPhillips carries, to this day, a scar. It is a kind of fetching little scar ... really a lovely little heart-shaped thing, don't you know?

VEGGIES

CHEESY POTATOES

8 or 9 medium potatoes
1 C. shredded cheese
Salt & pepper, to taste

1 can mushroom soup
1 C. milk

Cut potatoes, real thin. Put in large bowl. Add soup, milk and cheese. Put in oven and bake until potatoes are tender.

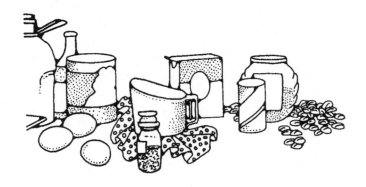

ZUCCHINI CASSEROLE

2 med. zucchini, sliced
Green pepper
1 can celery soup

½ or whole onion, diced
1 C. cracker crumbs

Sprinkle over top mozzarella cheese. Bake at 325° for 45 minutes. Sprinkle over top ½ lb. of hamburger (browned), draining grease. Bake 15 minutes more.

YUMMY POTATOES

1 2-lb. bag frozen hash browns
1 can cream of chicken soup
2 C. grated cheese

½ C. crushed corn flakes
¼ C. butter
1 pt. sour cream with chives

Layer potatoes in a 9 x 13-inch pan. Top with melted butter. Mix soup and sour cream. Spread on potatoes. Sprinkle with cheese. Mix melted butter and crushed corn flakes. Sprinkle on top. Bake at 350° for 1¼ hours.

SPINACH SOUFFLE (Serves 24)

20 oz. pkg. frozen, chopped spinach   1 T. salt
¾ C. flour   1½ lb. cottage chese
3/8 C. melted butter   2 C. American cheese (grated)
6 eggs, beaten

Mix all ingredients together and bake in 9 x 13-inch pan in moderate oven until set and spinach is done.

QUICK SCALLOPED POTATOES

2 T. oleo   6 C. sliced raw potatoes
2 T. flour   Onion flakes
2 tsp. salt   American cheese
2 C. milk

Melt butter in saucepan, stir in flour and salt; add milk, slowly stirring until sauce boils and thickens. Add potatoes, onion flakes (if desired) and cheese (what you like). Heat, stirring occasionally until sauce boils. Put in a shallow greased baking dish. Bake, uncovered at 350° for 35 to 40 minutes. This method will keep potatoes from curdling.

CREAMED CORN

2 T. sugar   1 tsp. salt
2 T. flour   ¼ C. milk
2 beaten eggs   ¼ lb. Velveeta
2 T. oleo   2 cans creamed corn

Mix and bake 45 minutes at 325°.

TUMERIC CABBAGE

4 qt. shredded cabbage (about 4 lbs.)   2 C. vinegar
4 onions, sliced   5 C. sugar
2 C. water   1 T. tumeric
1 T. celery seed   3 T. mustard seed
3 T. salt
   Bring dressing ingredients to a boil and pour boiling hot over the cabbage and onions. Store in the refrigerator in a covered container. This will keep several weeks. May use less onion if you prefer.

BROCCOLI CASSEROLE

1 pkg. frozen chopped broccoli   ½ C. Cheez Whiz
1 can cream of chicken soup   ½ C. water
1 C. instant rice
   Cook broccoli until tender. Add to other ingredients. Pour in casserole. Top with buttered crumbs or crushed potato chips. Bake at 350° for 45 minutes.

BAKED BEETS

1 (No. 303) can beets   2 T. brown sugar
2 T. butter   1 tsp. salt
2 T. flour   1½ T. horseradish
   Drain beets and add enough water to make 1 C. liquid. Melt 2 T. butter in saucepan. Add 2 T. flour. Stir until well blended. Add beet liquid. Cook until mixture begins to thicken, stirring constantly. Add 2 T. brown sugar, 1 tsp. salt and 1½ T. horseradish. Add drained beets. Pour into buttered casserole. Sprinkle bread crumbs over top. Bake at 375° for about 20 minutes or until crumbs are crisp and brown.

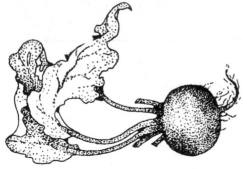

BAKED BEANS

1 large can pork & beans	2 T. vinegar
1 #2 can lima beans	½ tsp. prepared mustard
1 #2 can kidney beans	½ lb. bacon (1'' pieces)
1 #2 can butter beans	¼ C. catsup
1 C. brown sugar	½ medium onion (chopped)

Drain all beans, mix all ingredients and bake for 4 hours at 325°.

AUGRATIN CARROTS

4 C. cooked & sliced carrots
1 can cream of celery soup
1 C. shredded process cheese

¼ C. bread crumbs
1 T. butter (melted)

Combine carrots, soup and cheese in a 1 quart casserole dish. Combine bread crumbs and butter. Sprinkle over top of carrots. Bake at 350° for 25 minutes. 6 to 8 servings.

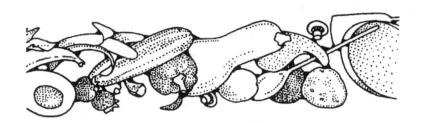

EASY GARDEN VEGETABLE PIE

2 C. chopped fresh broccoli or cauliflower
½ C. chopped onions
1 C. (4 ozs.) shredded cheese (or more)
1½ C. milk
¾ C. Bisquick baking mix

3 eggs
1 tsp. salt
¼ tsp. pepper
½ C. chopped green pepper & mushrooms

Heat oven to 400°. Lightly grease a 10-inch pie pan. Heat salted water to boiling. Add broccoli or cauliflower and cook for about 5 minutes. Drain thoroughly. Mix broccoli, onion, green pepper, mushrooms and cheese in pie plate. Beat remaining ingredients for 1 minute on high speed. Pour into pie plate. Bake until a knife inserted comes out clean, 35-40 minutes. Let stand 5 minutes before cutting. 6 servings.

CORN PUDDING

3 slightly beaten eggs
2 C. drained, cooked or canned
   whole kernel corn
2 C. milk, scalded

⅓ C. finely chopped onion (opt.)
1 T. butter, melted
1 tsp. sugar
1 tsp. salt

   Combine ingredients, pour into greased 1½ quart casserole. Set in a shallow pan, fill pan to 1-inch with hot water. Bake at 350° for 40 to 45 minutes or until knife inserted in center comes out clean. Then let stand 10 minutes at room temperature (center will firm up). Makes 6 servings.

SUNSHINE CARROTS

7 or 8 med. carrots
1 T. brown sugar
1 tsp. cornstarch
¼ tsp. salt

¼ tsp. ground ginger
¼ C. orange juice
2 T. butter

   Slice carrots bias style and cook. In small saucepan combine sugar, cornstarch, ginger and salt. Add orange juice and cook stirring constantly till thickened and bubbly. Boil 1 minute, remove from heat and stir in butter. Pour over hot carrots, tossing to coat evenly. Garnish with parsley and orange twist if desired. Serves 6.

PARSLEY BUTTERED CARROTS

2 C. carrots (sliced into
   ⅓ to ½-inch pieces)

2 T. butter or margarine
1 T. parsley flakes

   Place butter in 1 quart casserole. Heat in microwave on full power for 30 to 45 seconds or until melted. Stir in carrots, and parsley flakes. Mix well. Cook in microwave, covered on full power for 6 minutes or until tender.

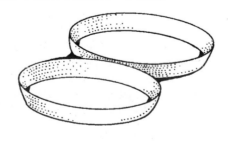

TEXAS POTATOES

4 C. diced boiled potatoes
1 C. minced onion
1 tsp. salt
½ C. chopped pimento
½ tsp. pepper

2 C. grated American cheese
2 C. medium white sauce
½ C. cracker crumbs
2 tsp. butter

Place diced vegetables in a greased casserole; add salt, pepper and cheese to hot white sauce. Pour over vegetables, top with crumbs and dot with butter. Bake at 350° until nicely browned, about 30 minutes.

STUFFED POTATOES

8 baking potatoes
½ medium onion (diced fine)
1 stick oleo

Salt
Pepper

In a 375° oven bake potatoes for 1 hour. Remove from oven and cut in half. Immediately spoon potato out of skin, being careful not to damage skin. In a bowl, add oleo and onion to potatoes; mash and beat until smooth. Add salt and pepper to taste. Spoon mixture back into skins. Place on a baking sheet and re-heat for 10 to 15 minutes.

POTATO CASSEROLE

6 medium potatoes
2 C. shredded Cheddar cheese
½ stick butter or margarine
2 C. room temperature sour cream

⅓ C. chopped green onion
1 tsp. salt
¼ tsp. white pepper
2 T. butter

Cook potatoes in skins. Let cool, then shred. Heat butter and Cheddar cheese until melted. Combine sour cream and green onions. Add salt, pepper and cheese mixture. Toss with potatoes. Dot with butter. Bake at 350° for 20-25 minutes in greased casserole.

SUPER-DUPER POTATOES

9 medium potatoes
½ C. butter
2 C. ½ & ½ cream

1 tsp. salt
8 ozs. shredded Cheddar cheese
Dried minced onion (to taste)

Cook, cool, peel and slice potatoes; about 1/8'' thick. Heat butter, cream and salt, until butter melts. Pour over the potatoes and cheese. Use a 9 x 13-inch pan. Bake 1 hour at 350°

OUCH

Speaking of fetching little scars in awkward places,
Edith Hawkin from over around Centerville learned the
hard way that just 'cause you decide to cook

some hottern'-all-get-out scalloped potatoes au naturale,
it doesn't mean it's a good idea to sit down and eat those
spuds with nuttin' on.

The word down at the bridge club was that Edith's chair
was supposed to have flown clean across the kitchen and
bounced off the far wall ... and the Hawkin house has a
long kitchen, too!

SOUPS

&

SANDWICHES

CABBAGE PATCH STEW

1 lb. hamburger	1 lb. can kidney beans, undrained
Salt & pepper, to taste	1 lb. can tomatoes, undrained
½ C. chopped onion	2 C. shredded cabbage
½ C. chopped celery	

Brown hamburger in electric frying pan; sprinkle with salt and pepper. Add onions and celery; cook for a few minutes longer. Add tomatoes; stir. Place cabbage over top; salt slightly. Cover and simmer for 20-30 minutes. Chopped green pepper may also be added, if desired. Serve in soup bowls. Yield 4-6 servings.

SLOPPY JOES

Chopped onion	¼ tsp. chili powder
2 T. flour	2 T. brown sugar
1½ lb. hamburger	1 tsp. salt
1 T. shortening	1½ C. tomato juice
½ T. Worcestershire sauce	

Brown hamburger and onion in shortening. Add remaining ingredients and simmer 15 to 20 minutes.

BEST-EVER BURGERS

1 egg
1 can (8 oz.) tomato sauce
1 T. diced onion flakes
1/8 tsp. dried garlic flakes
2 lb. ground beef

Salt & pepper, to taste
8 hamburger buns
8 slices American, Swiss or
    Cheddar cheese (optional)

In a large bowl, beat the egg and then add the tomato sauce. Stir in bread crumbs, onion and garlic. Crumble the ground beef into the tomato mixture. Sprinkle with salt and pepper and mix well, using your hands. Form into 8 patties. Cook burgers over hot coals, turning twice. Just before burgers are done, place rolls on the grill and toast lightly. Put a burger on each bun, topping with a piece of cheese. Pour some Secret Sauce over each hamburger. (Serves 8).

SECRET SAUCE

⅔ C. catsup
2 T. brown sugar

2 T. yellow mustard
2 tsp. Worcestershire sauce

Combine all ingredients and heat in a saucepan. Serve hot over hamburgers.

OVEN BEEF STEW

1-2 lbs. chuck (cut in ½" pieces)
2 C. diced carrots
1-2 C. diced celery
1 onion, chopped
3-4 med. potatoes, chunked

1½ tsp. salt (optional)
1-2 T minute tapioca
Pepper
1 T. brown sugar
1-2 C. tomato juice

Put all in a large casserole or roaster with tight lid. Bake at 250° for 5-5½ hours without disturbing. Delicious served with garlic bread or corn bread.

BISCUIT BURGERS

1 lb. ground beef
1 (8 oz.) can pizza or spaghetti
 sauce
1 T. minced onions
¼ tsp. salt
¼ tsp. oregano

Pepper
1 C. shredded cheddar cheese
1 small can mushroom pieces
 (opt.)
2 cans crescent dinner rolls
Sesame seeds

Brown ground beef; add remaining ingredients (except cheese). Cool. Open rolls - lay out 8 rectangles. Pinch perforated edges of rolls together to prevent leaking. Put ⅓ to ½ C. mixture on each rectangle of dough. Top with cheese. Fold over, press edges together with fork. Brush tops with milk. Sprinkle on sesame seeds. Bake 15-20 minutes at 400°.

BBQ GROUND BEEF FOR BUNS

¼ C. lemon juice
½ C. vinegar
1 C. water
5 C. catsup

½ C. brown sugar
2 T. chopped onion
2 T. dry mustard
1 qt. celery (opt.)

Combine ingredients and heat thoroughly. Do not cook to soften celery. Brown 8-10 lbs. ground beef. Add 1½ T. salt and ½ C. flour to browned meat. Add sauce. Mix to meat mixture and simmer. Serves 50.

CHEESE-POTATO SOUP

6 C. potatoes (chopped)	6 tsp. instant chicken bouillon
3 C. onion (chopped)	8 oz. process cheese spread
4½ C. water	loaf (cut up, government
	cheese is the best)

Boil potatoes, onion, water, and instant bouillon until potatoes and onions are fork-tender, about 10 minutes. Place cheese, 2 C. potatoes, onions, and drain water from potatoes in blender. Blend until uniform consistency. Pour over remaining potatoes and onions.

5 HOUR STEW

2 lbs. beef stew meat	1 T. sugar in ½ C. water
6 carrots (cut up)	5 ribs celery (cut up)
3 potatoes (peeled and cut up)	1 large onion (cut in chunks)
4 T. minute tapioca	1 C. tomato juice
	Salt and pepper to taste

Mix all above and bake at 250° covered for 5 hours. No Peeking! Serves 6-8.

CAREFUL!!

A sub-clause of the law that says DON'T FRY BACON is that the nude cook needs to judicially avoid pressure cookers.

You know how much of a
head of steam of super
hot water those things will
build up.

Just thinking about that
jet of steam coming out of
a pressure cooker is enough
to make a person run for
two sets of clothes, a beach
towel, a winter coat, and
something for your head.

It is best just to avoid
pressure cookers altogether.

SALADS

SPRING GARDEN SALAD

1 large carton small curd cottage cheese   1 medium onion
1 medium green pepper   4 T. chopped or snipped chives
1 large carrot
    Finely grate pepper, carrot and onion. Add to cottage cheese with chives; chill. Serve on lettuce leaves or tomato shell.

MARINATED VEGETABLE SALAD

1 20-oz. pkg. frozen Cal. blend veg.   3 or 4 tomatoes (cut in wedges)
   (cauliflower, carrots, broccoli)   3 or 4 green onions (sliced)
3 stalks celery (sliced)   1 pkg. Hidden Valley dressing mix
½ lb. fresh mushrooms (sliced) or   ¼ C. vinegar
   1 can mushrooms (drained)   ⅔ C. salad oil
    Bring frozen vegetables to boil in small amount of salted water. Cook two minutes, just to par-cook, drain and cool. Add remaining vegetables, toss lightly. Combine the dry salad dressing mix with oil and vinegar. Mix well and set aside to blend flavors (about 20 minutes). Pour over vegetables when cool. Chill 24 hours or longer, mixing lightly two or three times during the period to blend well. Add salt and pepper to taste. Other vegetables can be added if desired. This salad keeps well for several weeks.

FRENCH DRESSING

1 C. oil
½ C. vinegar
1 T. garlic salt
4 T. paprika
⅔ C. catsup
    Put in quart jar and shake.

1 lemon (the juice)
4 T. grated onion
⅔ C. brown sugar
⅔ C. white sugar

COOKED SALAD DRESSING

3 T. sugar
1 tsp. salt
2 egg, yolks, beaten
¾ C. water
1 tsp. dry mustard

2 T. flour
½ tsp. paprika
½ C. vinegar
1 T. butter

    Stir together in saucepan sugar, salt, mustard, flour, paprika and egg. Add water and vinegar, stirring constantly. Cook until thick, stirring constantly. Remove from heat; add butter and stir. Pour into jar, cover and cool. Store in refrigerator. This is especially good with potato salad. Makes 1¼ cups.

BUTTERMILK AND HERB DRESSING

1 C. buttermilk
1 C. mayonnaise
½ tsp. garlic salt
½ tsp. dried chives
½ tsp. basil

½ tsp. parsley
½ tsp. paprika
½ tsp. celery salt
1 T. soy sauce

Mix and store in refrigerator. Will keep several weeks. Good on lettuce, fresh cauliflower, fresh broccoli, etc.

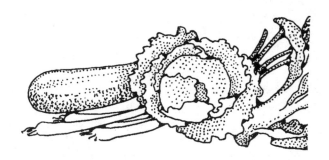

COLE SLAW DRESSING

2 C. Hellmann's real mayonnaise
1 can Eagle Brand milk

1 C. sugar
1 C. vinegar

Mix together and refrigerate. Will keep in a covered container for weeks.

POPPY SEED DRESSING

¾ C. sugar
1 tsp. dry mustard
⅓ grated onion
1 tsp. salt

⅓ C. vinegar
1 C. Wesson Oil
Poppy seed

Mix sugar, dry mustard, salt, onion and vinegar with a beater. Add Wesson Oil gradually and beat constantly. Add poppy seed. Keep in refrigerator.

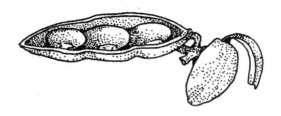

3 BEAN SALAD

1 15-oz. can garbanzo beans	¾ C. sugar
1 15-oz. can pinto beans	⅔ C. vinegar
1 lb. green beans	⅓ C. salad oil
½ C. sliced onion	1 tsp. salt
½ C. chopped green pepper	1 tsp. pepper

Turn garbanzo and pinto beans into colander and wash thoroughly. Then add the well drained cut green beans. Combine beans with onion and green pepper. Combine remaining ingredients and bring just to a boil. When completely chilled pour over the vegetables and toss lightly. Do not use until the following day, the longer this stands the better it tastes. Remember to stir it up from the bottom of the bowl whenever you open the refrigerator.

MACARONI SALAD

2 8-oz. pkg. curly macaroni (can sub.)	3 or 4 carrots (chopped)
1 green pepper (chopped)	2 stalks celery (chopped)
1 onion (chopped)	

DRESSING:

1 can Eagle Brand milk	1 C. white vinegar
1 C. sugar	1 pt. mayonnaise (no sub.)

Cook noodles until tender. Add chopped vegetables. Add dressing and chill for 4-8 hours before serving. Dressing also good on cole slaw.

CAULIFLOWER SALAD

1 head cauliflower
1 C. thinly sliced radishes
1 C. sliced carrots
1 C. chopped green peppers

1 C. sour cream
1 pkg. Good Seasons Farm Style
   dressing mix
¼ C. chopped green onions

    Separate raw cauliflower into flowerettes. Add radishes, carrots, green peppers and onion. Mix sour cream and dressing mix. Add to vegetables and stir to coat and chill.

FRESH CUCUMBER SALAD

2 pkg. lime Jello
1 can crushed pineapple
3 medium cucumbers, diced

½ C. Miracle Whip
½ C. whipped cream

    Prepare Jello with water, according to package directions. Add pineapple and cucumbers. Let set. Mix Miracle Whip and whipped cream and spread on top Jello.

KRAUT SALAD

1 qt. sauerkraut (glass jar preferred)
1 C. diced onion
1 C. green pepper, diced
2 C. sugar

⅓ C. salad oil
1 C. diced celery
2 cans red pimento

    Mix well and let stand overnight in refrigerator.

7 LAYER SALAD

1 lb. bacon, cooked
1 lb. frozen peas
½ C. onion
6 hard boiled eggs

1 head lettuce
Mayonnaise
Grated cheese

Layer by lettuce on bottom, chopped egg, peas, onion. Repeat above and top with mayonnaise and grated cheese.

HOT CHICKEN OR TURKEY SALAD

8 slices bread
2 C. chicken or turkey
½ C. chopped onion
1 C. chopped celery
½ C. mayonnaise

Salt & pepper, to taste
3 eggs
3 C. milk
1 can mushroom soup
Grated cheese

Tear 4 slices of bread into pieces, place in buttered 9 x 12-inch pan. Combine meat, onion, celery, mayonnaise and seasonings and spread over bread. Tear the rest of the bread into pieces and place over meat layer. Beat eggs and milk and pour over the mixture. Let stand overnight. Bake 1 hour at 350°. Then pour mushroom soup on top, sprinkling grated cheese over all. Bake 15 minutes more.

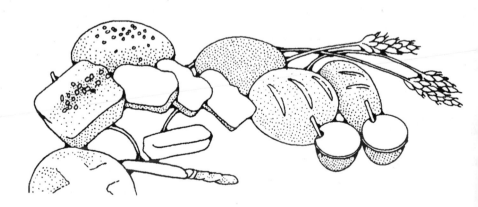

CORNED BEEF SALAD

2 pkg. lemon Jello
2 C. hot water
1½ C. Miracle Whip
2 tsp. vinegar
1 can corned beef

1 C. celery, chopped
3 boiled eggs, chopped
1 green pepper, chopped
Chopped olives
Chopped onion

   Dissolve Jello in water and cool. Separate corned beef with fork and add it with rest of ingredients to the Jello mixture. Let set.

GLAZED FRUIT SALAD

1 large can pineapple, drained & cut-up
1 or 2 cans mandarin oranges, drained
White grapes

Dark grapes
3 or 4 large bananas, sliced
2 T. lemon juice

   Drain canned fruit very thoroughly. Mix and chill for several hours. Better overnight. Fresh peaches, cantalope and watermelon may be added.

FLUFFY SALAD

1 24-oz. carton small curd cottage cheese
2 C. small marshmallows
1 3-oz. pkg. Jello

1 8-oz. carton Cool Whip
1 small can crushed pineapple
1 can mandarin oranges

   Put in large bowl and mix in order as given. Use whatever kind of Jello you like. This will keep covered in refrigerator for several days.

MOLDED CRANBERRY WALDORF SALAD

1 pkg. red raspberry Jello (3 oz.)
1 C. boiling water
1 can whole cranberry sauce
1 C. chopped apples

½ C. chopped nuts
½ C. chopped celery
1 C. cream, whipped

Dissolve Jello in hot water and chill. Fold in remaining ingredients and pour into mold.

5 CUP SALAD

1 C. drained pineapple (chunked)
1 C. bananas, sliced
¾ C. coconut

1 C. drained mandarin oranges
1 C. miniature marshmallows
1 C. sour cream

Mix together and chill.

FRUIT SALAD

2 or 3 oranges
½ C. sugar
1 T. lemon juice

1 No. 2 can pineapple tidbits
2 T. cornstarch
2 bananas, sliced

Peel and cut oranges into bite size pieces. Combine with pineapple and sugar and let stand overnight. Drain juice. Add lemon juice and cornstarch to drained juice, and cook until clear and thick; cool. Add to fruit and bananas and keep in refrigerator until serving time.

SALAD DRESSING

1 C. chili sauce
1 C. catsup
1 C. vinegar
   Shake well before using.

1 C. salad oil
1 C. sugar
Salt & dry mustard to taste

GOOD DRESSING

1 C. Mazola Oil
½ C. vinegar
½ C. sugar
1 C. catsup

¾ C. tomato paste
1 garlic clove or
   ¼ tsp. garlic powder

   Combine all ingredients and shake well; refrigerate.

GREEN AND WHITE SALAD

2 pkgs. lime Jello
1 pkg. lemon Jello
1 No. 2 can crushed pineapple
½ pt. whipped cream

1 small pkg. cream cheese
2½ C. boiling water
1½ C. boiling water

   Dissolve lime Jello in 2½ C. boiling water. Add pineapple and chill until set. Dissolve lemon Jello in 1½ C. boiling water. Add cream cheese. Beat with mixer. Chill till nearly set. Add whipped cream, pour mixture over lime layer. Return to refrigerator to set before serving.

RUSSIAN SALAD DRESSING

1 C. sugar   ½ C. vinegar
2 C. catsup   Juice of 2 lemons
1 C. salad oil   1 onion (minced)
   Mix all ingredients and store in covered jar in refrigerator. Shake well before using. Makes 2 pints.

MARSHMALLOW AND PINEAPPLE SALAD

1 large pkg. cream cheese   1 lg. pkg. marshmallows
¼ C. salad dressing   ½ pt. whipping cream
1 C. crushed pineapple
   Cream together cheese and salad dressing; set aside. Mix pineapple and marshmallows. Add this to cheese mixture. Whip whipping cream and fold into mixture. Mold or bowl. For a variety add coconut.

WESTERN DRESSING

1 C. sugar   1 T. onion
1 C. oil   1 clove garlic (diced)
½ C. vinegar   Salt, to taste
1 tsp. Worcestershire sauce
   Blend to smooth. Makes 1 quart.

DINNER SALAD

1 (3 oz.) pkg. lime Jello
1 #2 can pineapple (crushed)
1 C. grated carrots
1 C. chopped pecans

½ pt. whipping cream
¼ C. sugar
Dash of salt
1 C. grated Cheddar cheese

Heat pineapple to boiling and pour over Jello. Add sugar and salt. Let cool to set, then add carrots, cheese and pecans. Whip whipping cream and fold in above mixture. Fits nicely in a 7½ x 12-inch glass Pyrex dish; refrigerate.

FINGER JELLO

3 (3 oz. ea.) pkgs. Jello (any flavor)
4 env. Knox gelatin

4 C. boiling water

Dissolve Jello in water. Pour in 9 x 13-inch pan and chill until firm. Cut into squares. No need to refrigerate.

GOOD SALAD

1 can fruit juice cocktail
1 can crushed pineapple (drained)

1 can mandarin oranges (drained)

Mix together and add 1 (4 oz.) box of lemon pudding mix and refrigerate.

BASIC KNOX BLOX

4 env. unflavored gelatin   4 C. boiling water
3 (3 oz. ea.) pkgs. flavored gelatin
    In a large bowl, combine gelatins; add boiling water and stir till gelatin
dissolves. Pour into large shallow pan. Chill until firm. Cut into desired shapes.
Makes about 100 1-inch squares.

5 CUP SALAD

1 C. mandarin oranges   1 C. pineapple cubes
1 C. coconut   1 C. sour cream
1 C. miniature marshmallows
    Mix all together and serve.

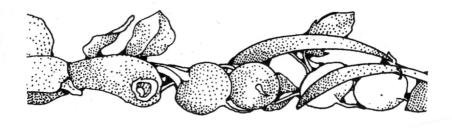

NEBRASKA FRUIT SALAD

1 can fruit cocktail (drained)   1 pkg. Dream Whip
1 can mandarin oranges (drained)   1 pkg. Instant vanilla pudding
1 or 2 sliced bananas
    Prepare Dream Whip and pudding as directed on package. Combine the two and
pour over fruit. Toss together.

MOLDED AMBROSIA SALAD

1 (3¼ oz.) can pineapple tidbits   1 C. sour cream
11 oz. can mandarin oranges   1 C. miniature marshmallows
6 oz. pkg. orange gelatin   ½ C. shredded coconut

    Drain pineapple and oranges; add enough water to juices to make 2 cups. Bring to a boil and stir in orange Jello. Chill until syrupy. Stir in sour cream thoroughly. Fold in fruit, marshmallows and coconut. Turn into greased 1 quart mold and chill until firm. Unmold and if desired, garnish with additional pineapple or mandarin oranges. Makes 6 servings.

GRANDMA ROSS' SALAD

1 glass pimento (cheese spread)   1 pkg. Dream Whip
1 small can pineapple (crushed)   4 C. marshmallows

    Cream together pimento cheese spread and crushed pineapple. Add Dream Whip (prepared according to directions on package), and marshmallows. Pour into cake pan or leave in bowl.

INSTANT SALAD

1 (12 oz.) carton cottage cheese   1 can drained pineapple
1 (3 oz.) pkg. Jello   1 carton Cool Whip
    Mix well and refrigerate.

MOUNTAIN DEW SALAD

1 large pkg. lemon or lime Jello
2 C. hot water
1 can Mountain Dew

1 large can crushed pineapple
  (undrained)
1 can lemon pie filling
1 (9 oz.) container Cool Whip

Mix together Jello, water, Mountain Dew and pineapple. Let this set. Spread lemon pie filling and Cool Whip over top; refrigerate.

ORANGE SALAD

1 (3 oz.) pkg. orange Jello
1 box vanilla tapioca pudding
1 box vanilla pudding

3 C. water (use juice from oranges)
1 (4½ oz.) pkg. whipped topping
2 cans mandarin oranges

Cook the above puddings, water and Jello until thick; let cool. Mix the remaining ingredients with the pudding mixture. Pour in salad dish and refrigerate.

PURPLE LADY SALAD

2 (3 oz. ea.) pkgs. black raspberry Jello
1½ C. boiling water
1 can blueberries (undrained)

1 (13½ oz.) can crushed pineapple
  (undrained)
2 pkgs. prepared Lucky Whip

Mix Jello with boiling water. Add blueberries and pineapple. Let set until partially set. Add Lucky Whip and stir gently. Pour into a pretty glass bowl and chill.

RASPBERRY SALAD

2 (3 oz. ea.) raspberry Jello
1 C. applesauce
2 pkgs. frozen raspberries
2 T. lemon juice
2¼ C. boiling water

Dissolve Jello in boiling water. When Jello has cooled off, stir in applesauce, thawed raspberries (with juice) and lemon juice. Chill until firm.

SEA FOAM SALAD

1 (3 oz.) pkg. lime Jello
2 (3 oz. ea.) pkgs. cream cheese
2 T. cream or canned milk
1 large can pears (drained)
1 C. pear syrup
1 pkg. Dream Whip (prepared)

Dissolve Jello in boiling pear syrup; cool. Mix cream cheese and milk in blender. Add Jello and pears, blending well. Fold into Dream Whip and chill.

FRENCH DRESSING

1 C. sugar
¼ C. salad oil
½ C. cider vinegar
1 C. catsup
1 T. grated onion
1/8 tsp. minced garlic
1 tsp. Worcestershire sauce

Blend all ingredients together until smooth.

GOOD SALAD

1 pkg. lemon Jello
1 C. hot water
1 C. apricot juice
1 C. diced canned apricots
1 C. cottage cheese

½ C. marachino cherries
1 pkg. Dream Whip
  (prepare according to directions)
Nuts

Dissolve Jello in hot water. Add juice, refrigerate until partially set. Add remaining ingredients and mix well. Sprinkle top with nuts.

RASPBERRY SALAD

1 (6 oz.) pkg. raspberry flavored gelatin
2 C. hot water
1 (15 oz.) can applesauce

1 (10 oz.) pkg. frozen raspberries
  (partially thawed)

Dissolve gelatin in hot water. Add applesauce and raspberries immediately. Stir gently to separate raspberries. Refrigerate in 1½ quart mold until firm. Unmold and serve. Serves 8.

SHAKE 'N BAKE

You know how it is with something you get to doing.
Everything seems to be going along at pretty much an
even keel, then something happens to test you. Something happens that makes you look deep into your own
soul and to come to a decision. That moment will often
cause you to chuck the whole thing.

Like in car racing. If you ever win The Big One, you'll find
it'll either re-inspire you to race with even more

enthusiasm, or you'll experience the reaching-of-the-top-
of-the-mountain syndrome, and the flavor of the race will
be gone.

Or maybe you take up horse riding. Everything is going
hunky dory until one day you get bucked off. That experience will either renew your dedication...and move you
to become an accomplished rider, or it will sour you on
hay burners for the rest of your life.

Within this context, the cookin-in-the-nude cook needs
to be aware of the Shake-and-Bake syndrome. It is the
feeling you get when you are innocently putting together
one of those recipes that involve putting something in a
sack and shaking the heck out of it to get that something
coated well with other goodies ... and inadvertently

catch a glimpse of yourself in the mirror.

That glimpse in the mirror can be the turning point in your career as a cook in the nude. The sight of yourself doing all that shaking and carrying-on can either make you decide you were a natural born cooker au naturale, or you'll give it up right on the spot.

Both extremes of response have been well documented. Agnus Smythe was so shocked at what she saw that she put her clothes back on right on the spot and never cooked sans clothes again.

On the other hand Mitzy Gordon liked what she saw so much that she'd go through the shaking and baking routine even for recipes that had nothing to do with that procedure.

Just thought I'd tell you about that.

MAIN DISHES

MEAT AND CHEESE LOAF

1 lb. ground beef
¾ C. diced onion
¼ C. chopped cheese
⅓ C. green pepper or pimento
1 tsp. salt
¼   tsp. pepper
    Bake at 350° for 1½ hours.

½ tsp. celery salt (scant)
¼ tsp. paprika
1½ C. evaporated milk
½ C. dry bread crumbs
1 egg

BAKED STEAK

1 can mushroom soup
½ bay leaf
½ clove garlic

1 T. Worcestershire sauce
⅔ C. water
½ onion, sliced

Flour round steak, season with salt and pepper. Brown and place in baking dish. Combine above ingredients. Heat in skillet and pour over meat and bake at 325° for 1½ hours.

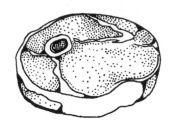

Ribs

SAUCE:
¾ C. brown sugar
¾ C. ketchup
1 T. vinegar

Nutmeg
Onion (med. size) browned

Brown ribs, pressure until tender, sprinkle nutmeg over mixture. Heat sauce in skillet. Add sauce and simmer 1½ hours.

TACO FRIED CHICKEN

1 env. taco seasoning mix
½ C. flour
¼ tsp. salt
1 egg, beaten

1 T. milk
1 frying chicken, cut up (2½-3 lbs.)
Shortening

Put taco mix, salt and flour in a bowl with a tight lid. Combine milk and egg in a bowl by themselves. Dip chicken in milk and egg mixture, then put in the bowl of seasoned flour. Put lid on and shake until the chicken is completely coated with flour. Then put in hot shortening and fry as you would any chicken.

CHOPS FOR HUNGRY CHAPS

6 pork chops
⅔ C. uncooked rice
1 C. water
2 tsp. salt

½ C. chopped onions
1 can (1 lb.) tomatoes (chopped)
1 C. whole kernel yellow corn
¼ tsp. black pepper

Trim some fat from chops. Fry out in a large skillet. Add chops and brown very slowly on both sides. Lift out. Pour off excess fat. Spread rice over bottom of skillet; add water. Sprinkle with 1 tsp. salt. Arrange chops over the rice. Sprinkle with the other 1 tsp. salt. Add the onions and tomatoes. Spoon on the corn. Sprinkle with the black pepper. Bring to a boil. Turn heat low. Cover and simmer 25 to 35 minutes or until the rice is tender. Add a small amount of water should mixture cook dry.

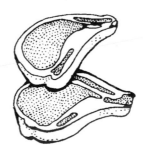

EGG ROLLS

1 lb. ground pork (do not brown)	1 T. soy sauce
1 T. onion powder	3 T. flour
1 T. garlic powder	2 eggs
½ tsp. black pepper	1 medium grated carrot
1 tsp. Accent	2 medium onions
1 tsp. salt	Need 2 pkg. egg rolls (cut in ¼ sq.)

Mix all above together and place 1 spoonful on each ¼ egg roll, deep fat fry until brown. Makes 1½ pkgs. of egg rolls.

SAUCE (To Dip Egg Rolls In):

1 C. white sugar	2 T. paprika
½ C. white vinegar	1 T. chopped green pepper
½ C. water	1 T. chopped pimento
½ T. cornstarch	

Boil above until dissolved well. Egg rolls are also good dipped in other types of sauce. Egg rolls may be frozen and reheated. They are best served hot but may be eaten cold.

CHAWAN MUSHI (Japanese)

4 eggs	3 oz. chicken, soaked 5 minutes in
2½ C. chicken broth	1 tsp. soy sauce
2 T. sake or wine	4 C. green beans (cooked & cut-up)
2 tsp. sugar	4 slices carrots
1 tsp. soy sauce	4 mushrooms (each cut in half)
2 tsp. salt	

Beat eggs well; add broth and mixture. Soak chicken in soy sauce. Divide chicken, beans, carrots, mushrooms into four oven proof cups (coffee cups work good). Pour the egg mixture over and cover with aluminum foil. Bowls are then set in a baking dish filled with water up to ⅓ to ½ of the height of the cups. Put i the oven at 350° to steam for 20-30 minutes or until custard is set.

MINI PIZZAS

2 loaves cocktail party rye bread
1 lb. ground beef
¾ lb. hot sausage
1 lb. Velveeta cheese

1 T. Worcestershire sauce
1 tsp. ground oregano
½ T. garlic powder
1 pkg. mozzarella cheese

Brown ground beef and sausage and drain; add cheese. Mix together Worcestershire sauce, oregano, garlic powder and mozzarella cheese. Add meat mixture and melt cheese over low heat. Spread on bread and place on cookie sheet and freeze. Then put in plastic bags and keep frozen until ready to use. Bake on cookie sheet at 350° for 10-15 minutes.

CALIFORNIA CASSEROLE

⅓ C. flour
1 tsp. paprika
2 lb. round steak, cubed
¼ C. shortening
½ tsp. salt

1 C. water
1 can cream of chicken soup
1¾ C. water
1 small can onions
1 small can whole carrots

DUMPLINGS:
2 C. flour
4 tsp. baking powder
½ tsp. salt
¼ C. melted butter
1 tsp. poultry seasoning
1 tsp. celery seed

1 tsp. onion flakes
1 T. poppy seed
¼ C. oil
1 C. milk
1 C. bread crumbs

Combine flour and paprika and use to coat meat. In pan, brown meat in shortening. Add salt, pepper and water. Simmer covered for about 30 minutes. Pour meat mixture into 13 x 9-inch baking dish. In same frying pan, bring soup and water to boil, stirring constantly. Combine with meat mixture. Add onions and carrots.

For Dumplings: Combine first 7 dumpling ingredients. Add oil and milk. Stir till moistened. Drop T. into crumb mixture. Roll and coat. Top casserole with dumplings. Bake uncovered at 425° for 20-25 minutes or until golden brown.

CHICKEN SUPREME

1 7-oz. pkg. creamettes macaroni
1 pt. milk
2 C. mushroom soup
1 onion, cut fine

½ lb. Velveeta cheese
(cut into small squares)
4 hard boiled eggs, diced
1 pt. cut-up chicken

Mix all ingredients together and leave in the refrigerator overnight. Take from refrigerate 2½ hours before putting into oven. Bake 1 hour or until golden brown in uncovered 9 x 13-inch dish at 350°.

? FOR TURKEY (Not Butterball)

1 stick butter
¼ C. oil
¼ C. white wine
1 tsp. salt
1 tsp. seasoned salt

2 oz. soy sauce
Dash garlic
Lemon juice
Liquid smoke

Mix all ingredients. Use big needle in syringe and inject all over turkey. Makes the meat super moist and great flavor.

GROUND PORK CASSEROLE

1 lb. ground pork
1 onion, chopped
1 can mixed vegetables

1 can tomato soup
1 pkg. mozzarella cheese

Brown ground pork and onion; drain. Stir in soup and drained vegetables. Bake for ½ hour at 350°. Top with cheese. Return to oven and brown till cheese melts.

CHICKEN ELEGANTE

3 large chicken breasts (skinned, boned
   & halved lengthwise)
6 thin slices boiled ham
6 thin slices mozzarella cheese
1 C. dry bread crumbs

½ C. Parmesan cheese
2 T. parsley flakes
¼ C. butter, melted
Sage

Place chicken breasts on cutting board and pound lightly with meat mallet to 5 x 5-inches. Place a ham slice and a slice of cheese on each cutlet, cutting to fit. Sprinkle lightly with sage. Roll up jelly roll style, pressing to seal well. Combine cream crumbs, Parmesan cheese and parsley. Dip chicken in butter, then roll in crumbs. Place in shallow baking pan. Bake at 350° for 40 to 45 minutes. Serves 6.

PIZZA

1 pkg. yeast
1½ C. warm water

3½-4 C. flour
½ tsp. salt

    Knead the above ingredients and let rise thirty minutes until double in size. Divide dough in half. Top with Ragu, cheese and toppings. Bake at 450° for 20-25 minutes.

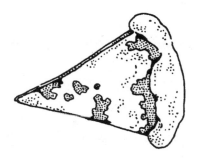

SPAGHETTI CASSEROLE

1 C. whole milk
1 tsp. butter
Salt
2 medium slices diced mild cheese

2 T. cream of celery soup
1 T. chopped onion
3 T. frozen chopped broccoli
2 C. cooked spaghetti

    Heat milk, butter and salt, but do not boil. Add cheese and let melt. Heat broccoli until thawed, remove from heat. Add milk mixture, soup and onion. Put cooked spaghetti in casserole and milk mixture, stir well mixed. Bake at 350°. Do not overbake and do not over cook spaghetti before pudding in casserole. Good hot or cold.

CHICKEN CASSEROLE

8 boned chicken breasts
8 bacon slices
1 C. chipped beef, rinsed & chopped

1 can mushroom soup
½ pt. sour cream

    Prepare day ahead. Wrap chicken breasts with bacon slices. Place chipped beef on bottom of casserole dish and put chicken breasts on top. Mix mushroom soup and sour cream together and pour over top. Refrigerate overnight. Bake at 275° for 3 hours.

TERIYAKI MARINADE

½ tsp. garlic salt   1 T. oil
1 T. brown sugar   2 T. water
½ tsp. ginger   ¼ C. soy sauce
½ tsp. black pepper   ½ tsp. Accent

Pierce meat every inch or so with meat fork and place in a covered container with marinade sauce. Turn occasionally. Soak overnight, or twelve hours. This is enough marinade for one round steak.

BARBECUED ROUND STEAK

1½ lb. round steak (1½" thick)   2 T. Worcestershire sauce
2 T. salad oil   ½ C. catsup
1 minced clove garlic   1 tsp. salt
¾ C. vinegar   1 tsp. dry mustard
1 T. sugar   1/8 tsp. pepper
1 tsp. paprika

Cut beef into crosswise slices 1" wide. Heat oil in skillet, brown steak strips on all sides. Remove meat to greased 1½ quart casserole. Pour off fat; place garlic and all remaining ingredients in skillet; simmer 3 minutes. Pour over beef; cover and bake in moderate oven 350° for 1 hour. Uncover and bake ½ hour. Makes 4 servings.

OVEN FRIED CHICKEN

Have cut-up chicken shake in a sack with pan cake mix, salt and pepper. Take out of sack and put in a pan for your size chicken pieces. Then put ½ C. of margarine all over the chicken. Then stick in oven for 30 minutes and check and turn oven at 350°. Then cook another 20 minutes or till done. Take out and serve hot. Can use juice for gravy.

FAVORITE QUICK SUPPER

MEASURE:
3 C. flour into large bowl. Answer telephone. Take large bowl off small son's head. Sweep up flour.

MEASURE:
3 C. flour into large bowl, ¼ C. shortening. Answer door bell. Wash shortening from son's hands and face.

ADD:
¼ C. shortening to flour, mix well. Rock crying baby 10 minutes. Answer telephone. Put son in tub and scrub well. Scrape flour and shortening mixture from floor, adding enough tears to relieve tension. Open 1 can of beans and serve with remaining strength.

EASY BARBECUED CHICKEN

2 T. Worcestershire sauce
1 tsp. salt
½ tsp. pepper
1 tsp. chill powder

¾ C. catsup
¾ C. water
3 T. minced onion
1 cut-up chicken

Mix together and bring to a boil. Pour over cut-up chicken. Place in oven at 350° for 2 hours or until done.

BARBEQUED CHICKEN FOR POTLUCK

3-3½ lbs. cut-up chicken
1 medium onion
2 T. fat
2 T. vinegar
2 T. brown sugar
¼ C. lemon juice

1 C. catsup
1 C. water
3 T. Worcestershire sauce
½ T. prepared mustard
½ C. chopped celery
Salt & pepper

Brown chicken and onion in fat. Add remaining ingredients and simmer for 30 minutes. Pour over chicken. Bake uncovered at 325° for 1 hour. Serves 6.

SALMON LOAF

1 can cream of celery soup	½ C. chopped onion
⅓ C. salad dressing	1 (16 oz.) can salmon
1 beaten egg	1 C. cracker crumbs

Drain and bone salmon; mix well. Bake in greased loaf pan at 350° for 1 hour.

ESCALLOPED SALMON

1 can salmon	2 eggs
1 can cream of chicken soup	1 C. cracker crumbs
½ C. milk	Salt & pepper
1 C. celery (chopped)	

Mix together well and pour into greased 8 x 8-inch baking dish. Bake at 350° for 45 minutes.

SEAFOOD STUFFING SUPREME

½ C. chopped celery
½ C. chopped onion
2 T. butter or margarine
1 can cream of shrimp soup
¼ C. milk
½ tsp. sage (crushed)

¼ tsp. dried thyme (crushed)
Dash of pepper
2 beaten eggs
4 C. dry French bread cubes
1 or 2 (4½ oz.) cans shrimp (drain)

   In a 3 quart saucepan, cook celery and onion in butter till tender, but not brown. Stir in soup, milk and seasoning. Add eggs, bread cubes and shrimp. Mix well and bake covered in 1½ quart casserole for 30 minutes at 350°. Uncover and bake 10 minutes more - garnish with parsley.

HAM CASSEROLE

1 stick butter
1 qt. milk
½ C. flour
1 lb. American cheese (cubed)
2 lbs. ground ham

3 T. horseradish
3 T. mustard
Dash of pepper
12 oz. pkg. noodles

   Cook until thick, the butter, milk and flour. Then add cheese, horseradish, mustard and pepper. Add ham and noodles to white sauce and place in 9 x 13-inch pan. Cook uncovered at 350° for 45 minutes. Can be made the night before. Serves about 20 people. Can be frozen.

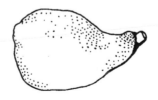

PORK KABOBS

3-4 lb. fresh ham roast
1 large onions (quartered)
2 large green peppers (cut-up)

4 med. firm tomatoes (quartered)
1 (4 oz.) can whole mushrooms

Cut roast in 1½'' to 2'' cubes. Alternate meat and vegetables on skewers starting and ending with meat. Grill over low heat for 1 hour and 15 minutes. Baste frequently with sauce. Serves 6-8.

SAUCE:
1 stick margarine
1 T. lemon juice

2 T. mustard

Heat until melted.

ROUND STEAK ROLL UPS

1 round steak
Prepared mustard
Bacon strips (uncooked)

1 pkg. dry onion soup mix
1 can golden mushroom soup

Pound round steak. Trim fat if necessary. Spread mustard on meat. Top with strips of bacon and sprinkle with dry onion soup mix. Roll up round steak and tie. Place on foil, cover rolled meat with golden mushroom soup. Wrap in foil. Bake at 325° for 3 hours. Save juices for gravy.

PORK CHOP CASSEROLE

5 thick chops
1 T. fat
Salt & pepper

1 #2 can cream corn
⅓ C. diced pepper
½ C. water

Brown chops slowly on both sides in fat. Sprinkle with salt and pepper. Mix corn and peppers and arrange in buttered casserole in alternately layers with chops. Add water, cover and bake at 350° for 45 minutes, then remove cover and bake 15 minutes longer.

EASY STEAK DINNER

1 pkg. onion soup mix (use dry soup mix)   1 can mushroom soup
1½ lb. round steak (1'' thick)
    Butter center of a 2½ ft. piece of aluminum foil. Sprinkle half the contents of the onion soup mix onto foil. Over this place the round steak. Top steak with remaining soup mix and dot with butter. Do not salt and pepper meat at all. Arrange soup around and over steak. Bring foil up and over meat, double edges to seal tight. Bake on cookie sheet at 375° for 1½ hours. Serve 4-6. When done, the meat has made sauce that goes well with potatoes.

GRAVY AND MEAT IN AN ELECTRIC SKILLET

Round steak or sirloin steak   1 small onion
2 T. shortening   3½ T. flour
3¾ C. water   ½ C. catsup
    Trim fat from steak. Cut into individual pieces. On low melt shortening, brown meat and onion. Remove meat; add flour. Mix well, turn skillet to 350° and add water. Mix well and add catsup. Boil and put meat back in and turn skillet down so gravy will be at a very slow boil. Stir and turn meat occasionally for 2 to 2½ hours. Before serving remove meat and bring back to full boil. Return meat and serve.

120

BEEF STROGANOFF

3 lbs. onions
2 lbs. round steak
6 ozs. tomato paste
1 tsp. Worcestershire sauce

⅓ C. fat
1 lb. mushrooms (sliced)
1 C. sour cream
Salt & pepper, to taste

Put the peeled onions through the food chopper. Drain and save juice. Heat the fat in heavy skillet. Add onions, cover and cook over low heat for 20 minutes. Add round steak, sliced very thin, mushrooms, salt and pepper; cook until brown. Add onion juice; tomato paste, sour cream and Worcestershire sauce. Stir well. Cover and simmer 1 hour, stirring occasionally. Serve with rice or noodles.

RICE MEATBALLS

1 C. raw minute rice
1 lb. ground beef
Dash of pepper
1 egg
2 tsp. grated onion

2½ C. tomato juice
2 tsp. salt
1/8 tsp. marjoram
½ tsp. sugar

Combine rice, meat, egg, onion, salt, pepper and marjaram and ½ C. of the tomato juice. Mix lightly and shape into balls and place in skillet. Add sugar to remaining tomato juice. Pour over meatballs in skillet. Bring mixture to boil. Reduce heat and simmer covered for 30 minutes. Baste occasionally.

MEATBALL SUPREME

1½ lbs. hamburger
½ C. milk
2 tsp. salt
½ tsp. pepper
1 C. catsup
½ C. water

¼ tsp. Worcestershire sauce
3 T. onions (chopped)
2 T. vinegar
⅓ C. brown sugar
Dash of Tobasco sauce

Mix hamburger, milk, salt and pepper. Shape into meatballs and brown. Combine remaining ingredients and bring to a boil. Place meatballs in casserole dish and cover with sauce. Bake in 325° oven for 1-1½ hours until sauce is thick.

FRENCH FRY CASSEROLE

1½ lb. ground beef
¼ C. onions, chopped
1½ lb. pkg. French fries

1 can cream corn
1 can cream of chicken soup
1 can cream of mushroom soup

Brown ground beef. Pour in soups and onions, cook a few minutes. Grease bottom of casserole dish. Place french fries on bottom of dish and pour mixture over french fries. Bake at 350° for 1 hour. Makes a large dish. Serve with hot bread or biscuits.

HAMBURGER CASSEROLE

1 lb. hamburger
2 C. whole corn, drained
Onion to taste

1 C. diced cheese
2 C. sliced potatoes
1 can tomato soup

Brown hamburger and drain off grease. In casserole dish, put corn, onion, cheese and potatoes. Add hamburger and soup. Stir this all up together. Bake for 1 hour and 35 minutes or until potatoes are done.

JUST WATCHING

wen Glaizer was a dyed-in-the-wool cooker in the nude for several years while they lived in the city. It was just one of those things that Gwen did.

But, things changed a lot after one day when her husband came home with the exciting news that he had gotten a promotion ...to branch manager of one of the company's outlying branch offices.

Of course, this meant the couple had to move. And the move was to a small town in a rural area near a large national forest.

It was a combination of things resulting from that promotion that caused Gwen to give up cooking in the nude.

You see, what with all that outdoors right at their back yard, Mark took up hunting. Oh, he'd gone out for a pheasant or two now and then throughout their married life. But this was different. It was excellent hunting and was just minutes from the house.

Almost as soon as they were settled in the new house, Mark got him a hunting dog,

and a new shotgun. Before long Mark was bringing game home on a regular basis.

Unfortunately, Mark was a lot better at shooting stuff than he was at helping to fix it, so Joyce got stuck with that job.

It wasn't that Gwen didn't want to fix all those goodies from the woods. In fact, she sort of enjoyed the challenge of learning how to prepare the various kinds of game her husband would proudly drag home.

But, slowly, a new realization occurred to Gwen. When she lived in the city, she would start a meal with plastic-wrapped turkey. Now she had to start with a no-parts-missing one.

While hamburger and steak came in very uncow-like form, her venison came complete with eyes.

Gwen came to realize that everything, in fact, she worked with had eyes.

Those eyes might have had the spark of life extinguished, but they appeared to be perfectly functional. There they would be, looking up at her from the floor or over at her from the counter top.

Gwen caught herself being more and more self-conscious when she was doing her kitchen chores in her birthday suit. Was that squirrel really looking at her? Was that buck deer as innocent as she knew him to be, deep in her heart?

The whole thing got to bothering Gwen more and more. It all sort of came to a boiling point when she was working at the stove and had the distinct impression she was being watched.

Gwen whipped around to observe an expired rabbit, looking like he had his eyes focused right on her! And, he seemed to have a silly grin on his face.

That was it!! Gwen delivered her ultimatum that very evening at supper. Either they go back to plastic-wrapped chicken and beef in one-pound packages, or Mark would have to do the wild game preparation thereafter.

Mark got pretty good at fixin' wild game.

DESSERTS

QUICK APPLE OR RHUBARB CRISP

5 or 6 apples (sliced) or   ½ C. water for apples
    about 3 C. chopped rhubarb   Cinnamon, to taste
1½ C. sugar for apples   1 stick of oleo
2 C. sugar for rhubarb   2 C. flour
½ tsp. salt   ½ C. sugar

   Slice apples or cut up rhubarb and place in the bottom of an 8 x 8-inch Pyrex dish. Fill half full. Sprinkle sugar and salt over fruit. Add water if using apples; none if using rhubarb. Sprinkle cinnamon to taste over top. In a bowl cut oleo into flour and mix in sugar. Mix well and pat down on top of fruit. Bake 40 minutes in 350° oven.

LEMON WALNUT FLUFF

1 pkg. lemon Jello   1 C. boiling water
1 C. brown sugar   1 C. water
1 C. chopped nuts   2 C. cream, whipped
Cherries

   Dissolve the Jello in the boiling water. Boil the brown sugar and water and add to first mixture; cool. When Jello begins to thicken beat until creamy and add nuts and whipped cream. Serve in sherbet glasses and top with a cherry.

MILLIONAIRES DESSERT

1 pkg. Jiffy yellow cake mix
1 pkg. pineapple cream instant pudding
1 9-oz. Cool Whip
Vanilla (optional)

8 oz. pkg. cream cheese, softened
2 C. milk
1 lg. can crushed pineapple
Flaked coconut (optional)

Bake cake as directed on package. Gradually mix pudding to softened cream cheese, then slowly add milk and a dash of vanilla if desired. Pour over cooled cake. Evenly distribute well drained pineapple over cheese mix. Top with Cool Whip. Sprinkle with flaked coconut if desired; refrigerate. Must be baked the day before for good cutting.

FRUIT PIZZA

CRUST:
1 C. margarine
1 egg
2½ C. flour
1 tsp. cream of tartar

1½ C. powdered sugar
1 tsp. vanilla
1 tsp. soda

TOPPING:
1 8-oz. pkg. cream cheese, softened
1 can mandarin oranges
Strawberries
Peaches
⅓ C. powdered sugar

1 can pineapple chunks
2 bananas (sliced & dipped
   in lemon juice)
1 C. apricot preserves

Mix the crust ingredients and chill. Roll thin to cover a pizza pan. Bake at 375° for 15 minutes; cool. Combine the softened cream cheese and powdered sugar. Spread over the cooled crust. Drain the fruits and arrange on top of the cream cheese mixture. Melt the apricot preserves and drizzle over the fruit. You may top with whipped cream just before serving.

STRAWBERRY DESSERT

CRUST:
1 C. flour   ¼ C. brown sugar
½ stick oleo   ¾ C. chopped nuts

MIDDLE LAYER:
30 big marshmallows   ⅔ C. milk
1 pkg. Dream Whip or 1 C. cream, whipped

TOP LAYER:
1 lg. pkg. or 2 sm. pkg. strawberry Jello   2 sm. pkg. frozen strawberries
2 C. boiling water

Cut the crust ingredients together like pie crust. Spread in 9 x 13-inch pan. Don't press in pan hard. Bake for 15 minutes at 350°; cool. Melt together the marshmallows with the milk, then cool and add 1 pkg. Dream Whip or whipped cream. Pour on top of the crust. Dissolve the Jello in boiling water and add the frozen strawberries. Cool and pour over the top; chill.

"BEST EVER HOMEMADE ICE CREAM"

10 eggs (well beaten)   4½ tsp. vanilla
3 C. sugar   ¾ tsp. lemon extract
Dash of salt   Milk to fill can
4 C. cream

Beat eggs, sugar and salt until light and fluffy. Add cream and flavorings; stir until well blended. Pour into freezer can and fill with milk to fill line. Makes 1½ gallons.

HOT FUDGE SAUCE

2 C. chocolate chips
3 C. miniature marshmallows
1 T. butter

1 large can Carnation milk
1 tsp. vanilla

Combine all ingredients in top of double boiler and heat until all is melted and smooth. Stir frequently. Serve warm. This may also be cooked in the microwave.

RHUBARB CRISP

3 C. rhubarb
1½ C. sugar
1 C. brown sugar
½ C. shortening
1 egg

1 C. flour
½ tsp. baking powder
¼ tsp. salt
½ C. milk

Mix together rhubarb and white sugar and pour into an 8 x 8-inch baking dish. Add brown sugar, shortening, egg, flour, baking powder, salt and milk in order and mix well. Spread over top of rhubarb mixture. Bake 45 minutes in 375° oven.

HOMEMADE ICE CREAM

1 pkg. unflavored gelatin
4 or 5 eggs (beaten)
3 C. sugar (split)
3 C. milk
½ tsp. salt

2 T. vanilla
2 C. cream
2 C. half & half
Milk to fill can

Soak gelatin in hot water. Beat eggs; add milk, salt and 1½ C. of sugar. Heat to scalding hot, remove from heat and add gelatin, an additional 1½ C. of sugar, cream, half & half and vanilla. Pour into freezer can and finish filling with milk. May add a little lemon flavoring if desired. Makes 1½ gallons.

GRAPENUT ICE CREAM

4 eggs, well beaten
1 qt. heavy cream
1 T maple flavoring
3 C. sugar

1 tsp. vanilla
1 C. grapenuts (soaked)
About 3 qt. milk

Beat eggs; add sugar, cream and flavorings. Soak the grapenuts a short time in some milk. Add grapenuts and about 3 quarts of milk. Mix together and pour into freezer can. Makes 1½ gallons.

NEED A GIFT?
For

- Shower • Birthday • Mother's Day •
  • Anniversary • Christmas •

Turn Page For Order Form
(Order NOW While Supply Lasts!)

TO ORDER COPIES

Please send me _____copies of **COOKING a la NUDE**

      Price per book $9.95

      Shipping and Handling $2.25

      Total .... _____

(Make checks payable to **Hearts 'N Tummies Cookbook Co.**)

Name_____

Street_____

City/State/Zip _____

Hearts 'N Tummies Cookbook Co.
3544 Blakslee St.
Wever, IA 52658
800-571-2665

TO ORDER COPIES

Please send me _____copies of **COOKING a la NUDE**

      Price per book $9.95

      Shipping and Handling $2.25

      Total .... _____

(Make checks payable to **Hearts 'N Tummies Cookbook Co.**)

Name_____

Street_____

City/State/Zip _____

Hearts 'N Tummies Cookbook Co.
3544 Blakslee St.
Wever, IA 52658
800-571-2665

Since you have enjoyed this book, perhaps you would be
interested in some of these others from **QUIXOTE PRESS.**

ARKANSAS BOOKS

ARKANSAS' ROADKILL COOKBOOK
    by Bruce Carlson ....paperback $7.95
REVENGE OF ROADKILL
    by Bruce Carlson ....paperback $7.95
LET'S US GO DOWN TO THE RIVER 'N...
    by Various Authors ....paperback $9.95
TALL TALES OF THE MISSISSIPPI RIVER
    by Dan Titus ....paperback $9.95
LOST & BURIED TREASURE OF THE MISSISSIPPI RIVER
    by Netha Bell & Gary Scholl ....paperback $9.95
TALES OF HACKETT'S CREEK
    by Dan Titus ....paperback $9.95
101 WAYS TO USE A DEAD RIVER FLY
    by Bruce Carlson ....paperback $7.95
VACANT LOT, SCHOOL YARD & BACK ALLEY GAMES
    by Various Authors ....paperback $9.95
HOW TO TALK MIDWESTERN
    by Robert Thomas ....paperback $7.95
ARKANSAS COOKIN'
    by Bruce Carlson ....(3x5) paperback $5.95

DAKOTA BOOKS

HOW TO TALK DAKOTA ....paperback $7.95
Some Pretty Tame, but Kinda Funny Stories About Early
DAKOTA LADIES-OF-THE-EVENING
    by Bruce Carlson ....paperback $9.95
SOUTH DAKOTA ROADKILL COOKBOOK
    by Bruce Carlson ....paperback $7.95

REVENGE OF ROADKILL
     by Bruce Carlson ....paperback $7.95
101 WAYS TO USE A DEAD RIVER FLY
     by Bruce Carlson ....paperback $7.95
LET'S US GO DOWN TO THE RIVER 'N...
     by Various Authors ....paperback $9.95
LOST & BURIED TREASURE OF THE MISSOURI RIVER
     by Netha Bell ....paperback $9.95
MAKIN' DO IN SOUTH DAKOTA
     by Various Authors ....paperback $9.95
THE DAKOTAS' VANSHING OUTHOUSE
     by Bruce Carlson ....paperback $9.95
VACANT LOT, SCHOOL YARD & BACK ALLEY GAMES
     by Various Authors ....paperback $9.95
HOW TO TALK MIDWESTERN
     by Robert Thomas ....paperback $7.95
DAKOTA COOKIN'
     by Bruce Carlson ....(3x5) paperback $5.95

ILLINOIS BOOKS

ILLINOIS COOKIN'
     by Bruce Carlson ....(3x5) paperback $5.95
THE VANISHING OUTHOUSE OF ILLINOIS
     by Bruce Carlson ....paperback $9.95
A FIELD GUIDE TO ILLINOIS' CRITTERS
     by Bruce Carlson ....paperback $7.95
Some Pretty Tame, but Kinda Funny Stories About Early
ILLINOIS LADIES-OF-THE-EVENING
     by Bruce Carlson ....paperback $9.95

ILLINOIS' ROADKILL COOKBOOK
by Bruce Carlson ....paperback $7.95
101 WAYS TO USE A DEAD RIVER FLY
by Bruce Carlson ....paperback $7.95
HOW TO TALK ILLINOIS
by Netha Bell ....paperback $7.95
TALL TALES OF THE MISSISSIPPI RIVER
by Dan Titus ....paperback $9.95
TALES OF HACKETT'S CREEK
by Dan Titus ....paperback $9.95
LOST & BURIED TREASURE OF THE MISSISSIPPI RIVER
by Netha Bell & Gary Scholl ....paperback $9.95
STRANGE FOLKS ALONG THE MISSISSIPPI
by Pat Wallace ....paperback $9.95
LET'S US GO DOWN TO THE RIVER 'N...
by Various Authors ....paperback $9.95
MISSISSIPPI RIVER PO' FOLK
by Pat Wallace ....paperback $9.95
GHOSTS OF THE MISSISSIPPI RIVER
(from Keokuk to St. Louis)
by Bruce Carlson ....paperback $9.95
GHOSTS OF THE MISSISSIPPI RIVER
(from Dubuque to Keokuk)
by Bruce Carlson ....paperback $9.95
MAKIN' DO IN ILLINOIS
by Various Authors ....paperback $9.95
MY VERY FIRST
by Various Authors ....paperback $9.95
VACANT LOT, SCHOOL YARD & BACK ALLEY GAMES
by Various Authors ....paperback $9.95
HOW TO TALK MIDWESTERN
by Robert Thomas ....paperback $7.95

INDIANA BOOKS

HOW TO TALK HOOSIER
    By Netha Bell .paperback $7.95
REVENGE OF ROADKILL
    by Bruce Carlson . . . . .paperback $7.95
LET'S US GO DOWN TO THE RIVER 'N...
    by Various Authors . . . . .paperback $9.95
101 WAYS TO USE A DEAD RIVER FLY
    by Bruce Carlson . . . . .paperback $7.95
VACANT LOT, SCHOOL YARD & BACK ALLEY GAMES
    by Various Authors . . . . .paperback $9.95
HOW TO TALK MIDWESTERN
    by Robert Thomas . . . . .paperback $7.95
INDIANA PRAIRIE SKIRTS
    by Bev Faaborg & Lois Brinkman . . . . .paperback $9.95
INDIANA COOKIN'
    by Bruce Carlson . . . .(3x5) paperback $5.95

IOWA BOOKS

IOWA COOKIN'
    by Bruce Carlson . . . .(3x5) paperback $5.95
IOWA'S ROADKILL COOKBOOK
    by Bruce Carlson . . . . .paperback $7.95
REVENGE OF ROADKILL
    by Bruce Carlson . . . . .paperback $7.95
GHOSTS OF THE AMANA COLONIES
    by Lori Erickson . . . . .paperback $9.95
GHOSTS OF THE IOWA GREAT LAKES
    by Bruce Carlson . . . . .paperback $9.95
GHOSTS OF THE MISSISSIPPI RIVER
(from Dubuque to Keokuk)
    by Bruce Carlson . . . . .paperback $9.95

GHOSTS OF THE MISSISSIPPI RIVER
(from Minneapolis to Dubuque)
    by Bruce Carlson ....paperback $9.95
GHOSTS OF POLK COUNTY, IOWA
    by Tom Welch ....paperback $9.95
TALES OF HACKETT'S CREEK
    by Dan Titus ....paperback $9.95
TALL TALES OF THE MISSISSIPPI RIVER
    by Dan Titus ....paperback $9.95
101 WAYS TO USE A DEAD RIVER FLY
    by Bruce Carlson ....paperback $7.95
LET'S US GO DOWN TO THE RIVER 'N...
    by Various Authors ....paperback $9.95
TRICKS WE PLAYED IN IOWA
    by Various Authors ....paperback $9.95
IOWA, THE LAND BETWEEN THE VOWELS
(farm boy stories from the early 1900s)
    by Bruce Carlson ....paperback $9.95
LOST & BURIED TREASURE OF THE MISSISSIPPI RIVER
    by Netha Bell & Gary Scholl ....paperback $9.95
Some Pretty Tame, but Kinda Funny Stories About Early
IOWA LADIES-OF-THE-EVENING
    by Bruce Carlson ....paperback $9.95
THE VANISHING OUTHOUSE OF IOWA
    by Bruce Carlson ....paperback $9.95
IOWA'S EARLY HOME REMEDIES
    by 26 Students at Wapello Elem. School ..paperback $9.95
IOWA - A JOURNEY IN A PROMISED LAND
    by Kathy Yoder ....paperback $16.95
LOST & BURIED TREASURE OF THE MISSOURI RIVER
    by Netha Bell ....paperback $9.95
FIELD GUIDE TO IOWA'S CRITTERS
    by Bruce Carlson ....paperback $7.95
OLD IOWA HOUSES, YOUNG LOVES
    by Bruce Carlson ....paperback $9.95

SKUNK RIVER ANTHOLOGY
    by Gene Olson . . . . .paperback $9.95
VACANT LOT, SCHOOL YARD & BACK ALLEY GAMES
    by Various Authors . . . . .paperback $9.95
HOW TO TALK MIDWESTERN
    by Robert Thomas . . . . .paperback $7.95

KANSAS BOOKS

HOW TO TALK KANSAS . . . . .paperback $7.95
STOPOVER IN KANSAS
    by Jon McAlpin .paperback $9.95
LET'S US GO DOWN TO THE RIVER 'N...
    by Various Authors . . . . .paperback $9.95
LOST & BURIED TREASURE OF THE MISSOURI RIVER
    by Netha Bell . . . . .paperback $9.95
101 WAYS TO USE A DEAD RIVER FLY
    by Bruce Carlson . . . . .paperback $7.95
VACANT LOT, SCHOOL YARD & BACK ALLEY GAMES
    by Various Authors . . . . .paperback $9.95
HOW TO TALK MIDWESTERN
    by Robert Thomas . . . . .paperback $7.95

KENTUCKY BOOKS

TALES OF HACKETT'S CREEK
    by Dan Titus . . . . .paperback $9.95
LOST & BURIED TREASURE OF THE MISSISSIPPI RIVER
    by Netha Bell & Gary Scholl . . . . .paperback $9.95
LET'S US GO DOWN TO THE RIVER 'N...
    by Various Authors . . . . .paperback $9.95

101 WAYS TO USE A DEAD RIVER FLY
     by Bruce Carlson . . . . .paperback $7.95
TALL TALES OF THE MISSISSIPPI RIVER
     by Dan Titus .paperback $9.95
MY VERY FIRST
     by Various Authors . . . . .paperback $9.95
VACANT LOT, SCHOOL YARD & BACK ALLEY GAMES
     by Various Authors . . . . .paperback $9.95

MICHIGAN BOOKS

MICHIGAN COOKIN'
     by Bruce Carlson . . . . .paperback $7.95
MICHIGAN'S ROADKILL COOKBOOK
     by Bruce Carlson . . . . .paperback $7.95
MICHIGAN'S VANISHING OUTHOUSE
     by Bruce Carlson . . . . .paperback $9.95

MINNESOTA BOOKS

MINNESOTA'S ROADKILL COOKBOOK
     by Bruce Carlson . . . . .paperback $7.95
REVENGE OF ROADKILL
     by Bruce Carlson . . . . .paperback $7.95
GHOSTS OF THE MISSISSIPPI RIVER
(from Minneapolis to Dubuque)
     by Bruce Carlson . . . . .paperback $9.95
LAKES COUNTRY COOKBOOK
     by Bruce Carlson . . . . .paperback $11.95

TALES OF HACKETT'S CREEK
        by Dan Titus . . . . .paperback $9.95
MINNESOTA'S VANISHING OUTHOUSE
        by Bruce Carlson . . . . .paperback $9.95
TALL TALES OF THE MISSISSIPPI RIVER
        by Dan Titus . . . . .paperback $9.95
Some Pretty Tame, but Kinda Funny Stories About Early
MINNESOTA LADIES-OF-THE-EVENING
        by Bruce Carlson . . . . .paperback $9.95
101 WAYS TO USE A DEAD RIVER FLY
        by Bruce Carlson . . . . .paperback $7.95
LOST & BURIED TEASURE OF THE MISSISSIPPI RIVER
        by Netha Bell & Gary Scholl . . . . .paperback $9.95
VACANT LOT, SCHOOL YARD & BACK ALLEY GAMES
        by Various Authors . . . . .paperback $9.95
HOW TO TALK MIDWESTERN
        by Robert Thomas . . . . .paperback $7.95
MINNESOTA COOKIN'
        by Bruce Carlson . . . .(3x5) paperback $5.95

MISSOURI BOOKS

MISSOURI COOKIN'
        by Bruce Carlson . . . .(3x5) paperback $5.95
MISSOURI'S ROADKILL COOKBOOK
        by Bruce Carlson . . . . .paperback $7.95
REVENGE OF THE ROADKILL
        by Bruce Carlson . . . . .paperback $7.95
LET'S US GO DOWN TO THE RIVER 'N...
        by Various Authors . . . . .paperback $9.95

LAKES COUNTRY COOKBOOK
        by Bruce Carlson ....paperback $11.95
101 WAYS TO USE A DEAD RIVER FLY
        by Bruce Carlson ....paperback $7.95
TALL TALES OF THE MISSISSIPPI RIVER
        by Dan Titus ....paperback $9.95
TALES OF HACKETT'S CREEK
        by Dan Titus ....paperback $9.95
STRANGE FOLKS ALONG THE MISSISSIPPI
        by Pat Wallace ....paperback $9.95
LOST AND BURIED TREASURE OF THE MISSOURI RIVER
        by Netha Bell ....paperback $9.95
HOW TO TALK MISSOURIAN
        by Bruce Carlson ....paperback $7.95
VACANT LOT, SCHOOL YARD & BACK ALLEY GAMES
        by Various Authors ....paperback $9.95
HOW TO TALK MIDWESTERN
        by Robert Thomas ....paperback $7.95
LOST & BURIED TREASURE OF THE MISSISSIPPI RIVER
        by Netha Bell & Gary Scholl ....paperback $9.95
MISSISSIPPI RIVER PO' FOLK
        by Pat Wallace ....paperback $9.95
Some Pretty Tame, but Kinda Funny Stories About Early
MISSOURI LADIES-OF-THE-EVENING
        by Bruce Carlson ....paperback $9.95
A FIELD GUIDE TO MISSOURI'S CRITTERS
        by Bruce Carlson ....paperback $7.95
EARLY MISSOURI HOME REMEDIES
        by Various Authors ....paperback $9.95
UNDERGROUND MISSOURI
        by Bruce Carlson ....paperpback $9.95
MISSISSIPPI RIVER COOKIN' BOOK
        by Bruce Carlson ....paperback $11.95

NEBRASKA BOOKS

LOST & BURIED TREASURE OF THE MISSOURI RIVER
by Netha Bell .... .paperback $9.95
101 WAYS TO USE A DEAD RIVER FLY
by Bruce Carlson .... .paperback $7.95
LET'S US GO DOWN TO THE RIVER 'N...
by Various Authors .... .paperback $9.95
HOW TO TALK MIDWESTERN
by Robert Thomas .... .paperback $7.95
VACANT LOT, SCHOOL YARD & BACK ALLEY GAMES
by Various Authors .... .paperback $9.95

TENNESSEE BOOKS

TALES OF HACKETT'S CREEK
by Dan Titus .... .paperback $9.95
TALL TALES OF THE MISSISSIPPI RIVER
by Dan Titus .... .paperback $9.95
UNSOLVED MYSTERIES OF THE MISSISSIPPI
by Netha Bell .... .paperback $9.95
LOST & BURIED TREASURE OF THE MISSISSIPPI RIVER
by Netha Bell & Gary Scholl .... .paperback $9.95
LET'S US GO DOWN TO THE RIVER 'N...
by Various Authors .... .paperback $9.95
101 WAYS TO USE A DEAD RIVER FLY
by Bruce Carlson .... .paperback $7.95
VACANT LOT, SCHOOL YARD & BACK ALLEY GAMES
by Various Authors .... .paperback $9.95

WISCONSIN

HOW TO TALK WISCONSIN . . . . .paperback $7.95
WISCONSIN COOKIN'
  by Bruce Carlson . . . .(3x5) paperback $5.95
WISCONSIN'S ROADKILL COOKBOOK
  by Bruce Carlson . . . . .paperback $7.95
REVENGE OF ROADKILL
  by Bruce Carlson . . . . .paperback $7.95
TALL TALES OF THE MISSISSIPPI RIVER
  by Dan Titus .paperback $9.95
LAKES COUNTRY COOKBOOK
  by Bruce Carlson . . . . .paperback $11.95
TALES OF HACKETT'S CREEK
  by Dan Titus .paperback $9.95
LET'S US GO DOWN TO THE RIVER 'N...
  by Various Authors . . . . .paperback $9.95
101 WAYS TO USE A DEAD RIVER FLY
  by Bruce Carlson . . . . .paperback $7.95
LOST & BURIED TREASURE OF THE MISSISSIPPI RIVER
  by Netha Bell & Gary Scholl . . . . .paperback $9.95
HOW TO TALK MIDWESTERN
  by Robert Thomas . . . . .paperback $7.95
VACANT LOT, SCHOOL YARD & BACK ALLEY GAMES
  by Various Authors . . . . .paperback $9.95
MY VERY FIRST
  by Various Authors . . . . .paperback $9.95
EARLY WISCONSIN HOME REMEDIES
  by Various Authors . . . . .paperback $9.95
THE VANISHING OUTHOUSE OF WISCONSIN
  by Bruce Carlson . . . . .paperback $9.95
GHOSTS OF DOOR COUNTY, WISCONSIN
  by Geri Rider .paperback $9.95

RIVER BOOKS

ON THE SHOULDERS OF A GIANT
  by M. Cody and D. Walker . . . . .paperback $9.95
SKUNK RIVER ANTHOLOGY
  by Gene "Will" Olson . . . . .paperback $9.95
JACK KING vs DETECTIVE MACKENZIE
  by Netha Bell .paperback $9.95
LOST & BURIED TREASURE OF THE MISSISSIPPI RIVER
  by Netha Bell & Gary Scholl . . . . .paperback $9.95
MISSISSIPPI RIVER PO' FOLK
  by Pat Wallace . . . . .paperback $9.95
STRANGE FOLKS ALONG THE MISSISSIPPI
  by Pat Wallace . . . . .paperback $9.95
TALES OF HACKETT'S CREEK
(1940s Mississippi River kids)
  by Dan Titus . . . . .paperback $9.95
101 WAYS TO USE A DEAD RIVER FLY
  by Bruce Carlson . . . . .paperback $7.95
LET'S US GO DOWN TO THE RIVER 'N...
  by Various Authors . . . . .paperback $9.95
LOST & BURIED TREASURE OF THE MISSOURI
  by Netha Bell .paperback $9.95
LIL' RED BOOK OF FISHING TIPS
  by Tom Hollatz . . . . .paperback $7.95

COOKBOOKS

THE BACK-TO-THE SUPPER TABLE COOKBOOK
  by Susie Babbington . . . . .paperback $11.95
THE COVERED BRIDGES COOKBOOK
  by Bruce Carlson . . . . .paperback $11.95
COUNTRY COOKING-RECIPES OF MY AMISH HERITAGE
  by Kathy Yoder . . . . .paperback $9.95
CIVIL WAR COOKIN', STORIES, 'N SUCH
  by Darlene Funkhouser . . . . .paperback $9.95

SOUTHERN HOMEMADE
     by Lorraine Lott . . . . .paperback $11.95
THE ORCHARD, BERRY PATCHES, AND GARDEN CKBK
     by Bruce Carlson . . . . .paperback $11.95
THE BODY SHOP COOKBOOK
     by Sherrill Wolff . . . . .paperback $14.95
CAMP COOKING COOKBOOK
     by Mary Ann Kerl . . . . .paperback $9.95
FARMERS' MARKET COOKBOOK
     by Bruce Carlson . . . . .paperback $9.95
HERBAL COOKERY
     by Dixie Stephen . . . . .paperback $9.95
MAD ABOUT GARLIC
     by Pat Reppert . . . . .paperback $9.95
BREADS! BREADS! BREADS!
     by Mary Ann Kerl . . . . .paperback $9.95
PUMPKIN PATCHES, PROVERBS & PIES
     by Cherie Reilly . . . . .paperback $9.95
ARIZONA COOKING
     by Barbara Soden . . . . .paperback $5.95
SOUTHWEST COOKING
     by Barbara Soden . . . . .paperback $5.95
EATIN' OHIO
     by Rus Pishnery . . . . .paperback $9.95
EATIN' ILLINOIS
     by Rus Pishnery . . . . .paperback $9.95
KENTUCKY COOKIN'
     by Marilyn Tucker Carlson . . . . .paperback $5.95
INDIANA COOKIN'
     by Bruce Carlson . . . . .paperback $5.95
KANSAS COOKIN'
     by Bruce Carlson . . . . .paperback $5.95

NEW JERSEY COOKING
by Bruce Carlson . . . . .paperback $5.95
NEW MEXICO COOKING
by Barbara Soden . . . . .paperback $5.95
NEW YORK COOKIN'
by Bruce Carlson . . . . .paperback $5.95
OHIO COOKIN'
by Bruce Carlson . . . . .paperback $5.95
PENNSYLVANIA COOKING
by Bruce Carlson . . . . .paperback $5.95
AMISH-MENNONITE STRAWBERRY COOKBOOK
by Alta Kauffman . . . . .paperback $5.95
APPLES! APPLES! APPLES!
by Melissa Mosley . . . . .paperback $5.95
APPLES GALORE!!!
by Bruce Carlson . . . . .paperback $5.95
BERRIES! BERRIES! BERRIES!
by Melissa Mosley . . . . .paperback $5.95
BERRIES GALORE!!!
by Bruce Carlson . . . . .paperback $5.95
CHERRIES! CHERRIES! CHERRIES!
by Marilyn Carlson . . . . .paperback $5.95
CITRUS! CITRUS! CITRUS!
by Lisa Nafziger . . . . .paperback $5.95
COOKING WITH CIDER
by Bruce Carlson . . . . .paperback $5.95
COOKING WITH THINGS THAT GO BAA
by Bruce Carlson . . . . .paperback $5.95
COOKING WITH THINGS THAT GO CLUCK
by Bruce Carlson . . . . .paperback $5.95
COOKING WITH THINGS THAT GO MOO
by Bruce Carlson . . . . .paperback $5.95
COOKING WITH THINGS THAT GO OINK
by Bruce Carlson . . . . .paperback $5.95

GARLIC! GARLIC! GARLIC!
    by Bruce Carlson . . . . .paperback $5.95
KID COOKIN'
    by Bev Faaborg . . . . .paperback $5.95
THE KID'S GARDEN FUN BOOK
    by Theresa McKeown . . . . .paperback $5.95
KID'S PUMPKIN FUN BOOK
    by J. Ballhagen . . . . .paperback $5.95
NUTS! NUTS! NUTS!
    by Melissa Mosley . . . . .paperback $5.95
PEACHES! PEACHES! PEACHES!
    by Melissa Mosley . . . . .paperback $5.95
PUMPKINS! PUMPKINS! PUMPKINS!
    by Melissa Mosley . . . . .paperback $5.95
VEGGIE-FRUIT-NUT MUFFIN RECIPES
    by Darlene Funkhouser . . . . .paperback $5.95
WORKING GIRL COOKING
    by Bruce Carlson . . . . .paperback $5.95
SOME LIKE IT HOT!!!
    by Barbara Soden . . . . .paperback $5.95
HOW TO COOK SALSA
    by Barbara Soden . . . . .paperback $5.95
COOKING WITH FRESH HERBS
    by Eleanor Wagner . . . . .paperback $5.95
BUFFALO COOKING
    by Momfeather . . . . .paperback $5.95
NO STOVE-NO SHARP KNIFE KIDS NO-COOK COOKBOOK
    by Timmy Denning . . . . .paperback $9.95

MISCELLANEOUS

HALLOWEEN
    by Bruce Carlson . . . . .paperback $9.95
VEGGIE TALK
    by Glynn Singleton . . . . .paperback $6.95
WASHASHORE
    by Margaret Potter . . . . .paperback $9.95
PRINCES AND TOADS
    by Dr. Sharon Tobler . . . . .paperback $12.95
HOW SOON CAN YOU GET HERE, DOC?
    by David Wynia, DVM . . . . .paperback $9.95
MY PAW WAS A GREAT DANE
    by R. E. Rasmussen, DVM . . . . .paperback $14.95

To order any of these books
from Quixote Press
call
1-800-571-2665

pg 71 Carrots
.74 Potatoes